Arist

Women

Wealth

Menander
The Malcontent
The Woman from Samos

Written in the century following the defeat of Athens by the Spartans in the Peloponnesian War, these four plays signal a change of emphasis in stage comedy more appropriate to the new world order of the fourth century BC.

Aristophanes is the only Greek playwright whose work spans the fifth and fourth centuries BC and links the direct slapstick and bawdy of Old Comedy to the more subtly situational New Comedy. *Women in Power* and *Wealth* complete the cycle of Aristophanes's extant plays begun in *Aristophanes Plays: One* and *Plays: Two*, translated by Kenneth McLeish. Writing seventy years after Aristophanes's death, Menander's only complete surviving works, *The Malcontent* and *The Women from Samos*, are here translated by J Michael Walton.

Kenneth McLeish and J Michael Walton provide full introductions; discussing the plays and placing them in their political and social context.

ARISTOPHANES & MENANDER

New Comedy

ARISTOPHANES

Women in Power (*Ekklesiazousai*)
Wealth

translated by Kenneth McLeish

MENANDER

The Malcontent
The Woman from Samos

translated by J Michael Walton

with introductions by J Michael Walton and Kenneth McLeish

METHUEN DRAMA

METHUEN WORLD CLASSICS

This collection first published in Great Britain 1994
by Methuen Drama
an imprint of Reed Consumer Books Ltd
Michelin House, 81 Fulham Road, London SW3 6RB
and Auckland, Melbourne, Singapore and Toronto
and distributed in the United States of America by Heinemann,
a division of Reed Publishing (USA) Inc, 361 Hanover Street,
Portsmouth, New Hampshire 03801 3959

Reprinted 1994

An earlier version of this translation of *Women in Power* was first
published in Great Britain in 1979 by Cambridge University Press.
Translation copyright © 1979, 1994 by Kenneth McLeish
Wealth translation copyright © 1994 by Kenneth McLeish
The Malcontent translation copyright © by J Michael Walton
The Woman from Samos translation copyright © by J Michael Walton
Copyright © in this collection 1994 by Methuen Drama
J Michael Walton's introduction copyright © 1994
by J Michael Walton
Kenneth McLeish's introduction copyright © 1994
by Kenneth McLeish

The translators have asserted their moral rights

ISBN 0–413–67180–1

A CIP catalogue record for this book
is available at the British Library

Typeset by Wilmaset Ltd, Birkenhead, Wirral
Printed and bound in Great Britain by
Cox & Wyman Ltd, Reading, Berkshire

CONTENTS

ARISTOPHANES & MENANDER

The Athenian defeat by the Spartans in 404 BC marked much more than an end to the Peloponnesian War which had been waged intermittently for the past twenty-seven years. The triumphant Spartans imposed humiliating conditions on a people proud of their independence. The navy was dismantled apart from twelve ships and the Long Walls between Athens and the Piraeus were demolished. While the songs of the victors were proclaiming the first day of Greek freedom, Athenian democracy was replaced by an oligarchy of the Thirty Tyrants. To the wounds of war were added the humiliation of peace, from which, some would say, Athens never recovered. A reign of civic terror ended in civil war with acts of personal revenge barely disguised as a political power struggle.

Amidst such mayhem, what happened to the theatre was hardly an issue to distract the historian. The death of the two great tragedians, Sophocles and Euripides, in 406 BC had already signified the end of an era. Aristophanes implied as much in his play *Frogs* produced at the Lenaia of 405 BC in which he set up a contest in Hades between the long-dead Aeschylus and new arrival Euripides to see which of the two should return to Athens. Aeschylus wins the competition in *Frogs*, less as the superior playwright – in theatrical matters Dionysus as judge cannot choose between the two – but because he has the better advice to offer on a political issue. 'What are we to do about Alcibiades?', asks Aristophanes through his dramatic mouthpiece, Dionysus. 'Don't trust him', advises Euripides, 'you've been let down too often'. 'You must', counters Aeschylus, 'there's no other hope'. Though these sentiments are couched in language more suitable for a comic denouement, they cannot but appear distillations of the most pressing of contemporary debates. Alcibiades, General, statesman and the sort of wayward genius around whose life blockbusters are set, was spending the last years of the war in one of his periods of exile from his native Athens.

The outcome of *Frogs* is that the advice of Aeschylus prevails and he is awarded a return trip from the dead in order to try and save the living Athens, presumably, if Aristophanes has his way, in tandem with the erratic Alcibiades. That is the theatre's answer, at least as delivered by the one great comic playwright from the period of Athens' supremacy. Sixty-seven years after Aeschylus had celebrated the Athenian victory over the Persian invaders in *Persians*, and thereby provided the European theatre with the foundation stone of its dramatic tradition, his shade made this ghostly return to wave farewell on behalf of political tragedy.

Had Aeschylus really returned at that point, it is unlikely that he could have made any difference, so far lost was the Athenian cause. With his uncompromising ideals, he would probably have fallen victim to the postwar purges as surely as did Socrates in 399 BC. The Athens of the last years of the fifth century was no longer the Athens which Aeschylus had trumpeted in his plays from the years of the struggle for democracy. The end of the war marked the end of an era.

The culture of the fifth century BC had never been part of a static system but the years of the Athenian empire were marked by a brashness and a boldness never recovered in the fourth century world of Plato and Demosthenes. In periods when political supremacy is matched by cultural imagination, the drama tends to serve as a social mirror. Aeschylus and Sophocles offer a picture of the world where mythical heroes accept responsibility for their own actions, for all it is a world over which a man has limited control, a woman virtually none. Fate is the ultimate arbiter, so unpredictable are the gods, but, if mortals go down, they go down fighting. Euripides parades a bleaker vision. Heroes with mean motives and cut-price bravado look less like Homeric supermen than shady politicians. Received with suspicion during his lifetime, Euripides' cynicism proved to have real appeal in the heyday of the orators and the philosophers, to such an extent that no fourth century festival was complete without a Euripides revival.

Aristophanes holds a special place in this period of political and social transition. He survived the last years of the Peloponnesian War and its chaotic aftermath. What is more he was still writing for the stage nearly twenty years after the death of Sophocles and Euripides, at a time when political stability had returned to Athens and the city was again getting embroiled in foreign alliance and intrigue.

To the fifth century he had supplied a comic dimension by building a world peopled with Gods, heroes, mythical beasts, actual Athenians – or at least their stage caricatures – and fictional Athenians real enough to be met in the nearest taverna. Through this gallimaufry of characters and a progression of situations, one part plausible to four anarchic, Aristophanes created a unique stage world. If the tragedian provided in Athens a remove from life through the dimension of myth, the comedian dived headfirst into political reality with the attendant risk of alienating some of his audience as he amused the rest.

Old Comedy was very much a fifth century phenomenon. Dozens of writers had had their comedies performed at the festivals of the Lenaia and the Great Dionysia from early in the fifth century. Only the plays of Aristophanes have survived in written text but the consensus was at the time and later that as a comedian he was way ahead of his rivals. Nine of his plays appear in the two companion volumes, *Aristophanes Plays: One* and *Aristophanes Plays: Two*, from *Acharnians* of 425 BC to *Frogs* of 405. All these nine contain the same heady mix of fantasy and farce, spiced with social satire and politics together with an edge from the war hard enough to make an audience wince at a remove of two and a half thousand years.

That might have seemed to be the end of the story with Aristophanes bowing out at the right time before Athens finally cracked and the world went mad. But Aristophanes survived the defeat by the Spartans. He survived the rule of the Thirty Tyrants and saw the restoration of democracy and the birth of a new world, less direct and more subtle. He went on writing and producing plays, from amongst which *Ekklesiazousai* or *Women in Power* from 392 BC and *Ploutos* or *Wealth* from 388 are the sole survivors. Between them these last two plays show a change of emphasis in stage comedy, making it more appropriate for the new century. In the process Aristophanes created a form which represents far better than do his earlier nine plays the true beginning of the European comic tradition.

With his death, probably a couple of years after *Wealth*, Aristophanes, the political and social pundit, passed largely from the public view, disqualified from revival initially by his parochialism, later by the squeamishness of generations uncomfortable with his scatological and sexual exuberance. *Women in Power* and especially *Wealth* did find some favour by being accessible to other ages. Influence and affluence, their central themes, will remain among the most popular topics for debate until the unlikely dawn of a society where reward matches merit.

Wealth does possess its superhuman level in the figures of Wealth himself, both god and abstract, and in the monstrous Poverty, but the world of Athenian politics is practically invisible. The emphasis instead is on the individual. A new spirit of realism is abroad, first hinted at in the romance plays of Euripides, but looking forward to the pure social satire of comedy to come. Though Menander, who did not begin writing for the stage until Aristophanes had been dead for sixty years, is the true new broom, the turn of the century from fifth to fourth marks a point of no return. Comedy leaves hometown Athens and sets out to seek its fortune in the world. Hence the decision to present Aristophanes' last two plays in the present volume in tandem with the two surviving Menanders.

Aristophanes' late plays show a change in the function and conduct of dramatic performance which New Comedy will confirm. The new secularism is typified by the Prologue of

Menander's *The Malcontent*, delivered by the god Pan, less a figure of supernatural than of authorial status. The more mature *The Woman from Samos* lacks even token paternalism as the retreat of the gods from responsibility for human affairs turns into a rout.

Though such a change of emphasis in Menander was long suspected, not until the last century has it been possible to make an informed judgement. A reputation amongst Hellenistic and Roman commentators, higher than that of any other comic writer of antiquity, had to be taken on trust. Not a single Menander play had survived the dark ages and only enough fragments to whet the appetite. The unearthing at the beginning of the present century of a number of papyri in Egypt led to the publication of substantial portions of three plays in 1907, one of them *Samia*, *The Woman from Samos*. In 1955 a whole play turned up, *Duskolos*, *The Bad-Tempered Man*, here translated as *The Malcontent*, together with more bits of *The Woman from Samos* and other sections of text which were not published until 1969. Much of the rediscovered material came from scripts that had been used for covering mummies, a process of transmission so eccentric it can only lead to the hope that there may be more plays still to come to light.

A reputation based largely on quotation and hearsay now had some substance and *The Woman from Samos* is sufficiently complete for the present translator to have supplied the missing hundred and thirty or so lines without having to invent plot or, hopefully, compromise characters. What the play reveals is a limited but acute view of a society whose published or publishable concerns are those of family relationships, social and, at arm's length, sexual intercourse: and not much else. The reader who wants to know about the political structure of post-Alexander Athens might as profitably study the mummy as the mummy-case.

Menander as a man remains an elusive figure, an Athenian and a philosopher, but a playwright whose work lacks any of the autobiographical touches that illuminate Aristophanes. The Athens in which he lived was dominated by Macedon and his friendship with Demetrius of Phalerum, governor of Athens from 317–307 BC, may have made him an object of suspicion, especially after Demetrius was removed from power when Menander was in his mid-thirties. Whatever his popularity during his lifetime, it was an ability to tune in to common human experience in his plays which underpinned his reputation in the centuries following his death.

Apart from the last two plays of Aristophanes and the only surviving two of Menander, which comprise the present volume, the remainder of classical comedy is represented exclusively by plays in Latin written, for the most part, a hundred years after Menander died. Even to mention them in this context might seem superfluous were it not for two factors which serve to highlight the superiority of the Greek originals as well as the difference between Aristophanes and Menander.

Roman drama had a history that went back to before Menander's birth, but any independent growth was stifled by its Greek antecedents. Roman tragedy from republican times, as far as may be gleaned from the mercifully short surviving fragments, was turgid or derivative, or both. Comedy, for which the Romans had a greater flair, was either localised to various parts of Italy or, again, borrowed from Greece. The stage of Plautus and Terence is a place where the issues, as in Menander, are issues of human relationships, fathers and sons, arranged marriages, the status of cooks and pimps. What in other eras would point to a unique glimpse of parish politics is obscured in Latin New Comedy by one prime consideration. None of the plays of Plautus or Terence is truly original. None is truly Roman. All are adaptations of plays written in Greek by Greek playwrights up to a hundred and fifty years before the time in which they appear to be set. It is as though a Tom Stoppard play based on Schnitzler or Molnar was not a welcome novelty on the contemporary stage but the staple diet. The pedigree of being Greek is positively paraded as a guarantee of quality. Nobody would dispute that there are original features in both Plautus and Terence but equally noone would suggest that setting, plot, or, for the most part, character are among these features.

The prologues of Plautus and Terence are a mine of information, revealing, as they do, the backbiting and petty jealousies to which the theatre seems ever heir. They also contain spirited and revealing details of how the playwrights treated their Greek originals. Terence confesses to, or rather prides himself in, having borrowed almost all his work from Menander and Diphilus, while Plautus raided the whole range of Middle Comedy back to before Menander was born. What neither showed any interest in was Aristophanes whose latterday conversion to social concerns was still too individual to travel to another country and another century. Plautus and Terence were 'Greekish' and their stage worlds rooted in the Hellenistic Menander. Aristophanes was the old world, steadfastly Athenian, writing even in the twilight of his career for an audience to whom Athens was still, if only just, the centre of the civilised world.

The sheer exuberance of the younger Aristophanes was well suited to the theatrical conditions of the fifth century. The open-air Theatre of Dionysus had been modified and improved at the instigation of Pericles as part of the building programme which renewed the Acropolis. Pericles was not to live to see the theatre precinct completed. He died in the early years of the Peloponnesian War, some three years before Aristophanes first wrote for the theatre. Possibly as a result of the war the construction work took a further ten years. The completed Precinct of Dionysus on the south-eastern side of the Acropolis included a permanent *theatron*, or auditorium, set into the natural slope of the hillside. Here a massive audience of at least fifteen thousand – Plato believed they could number thirty thousand – looked down from a steep rake to the dancing-place below. The dancing-place or *orchestra* was the home of the chorus who featured so prominently in the tragedies of Aeschylus, Sophocles and Euripides, as well as in the fifth century comedies of Aristophanes. *Theatron* and *orchestra* were permanent in the sense that their shape and size were dictated by the natural bowl shape of the site, with the *orchestra* bounded by seats around two-thirds of its circumference. Behind the *orchestra*, from the audience viewpoint, was the performance space for actors and any scene-building or scenery. This part of the theatre was impermanent and variable.

By the closing years of the fifth century the scene building, or *skene*, was of substantial size, with a door or doors, an accessible roof and stage machinery including a platform which could be wheeled out for reveals and tableaux, the *ekkuklema*, and a stage crane, the *mechane*, for introducing celestial figures over the top of the action. Aristophanes has great fun with such devices, by drawing attention to their patent theatricality within his plays. Solid and dependable as such scenic devices had to be, the *skene* was not a permanent structure. The background was wood, as was the raised stage, if there was one, and any decorative features or scenic units. The arguments over how much was represented and how much left to the imagination of the audience still rage and are unlikely to be resolved. A reading of the plays written for this theatre space, tragedies, satyr plays and comedies, points to a need for flexibility and a background which at the very least framed the masked actors and exploited their physical relationship with chorus and audience. Most modern readings of the theatrical context in Athens point to a common sign system, independent of, but associated with, that found in the other visual arts of the period.

Women in Power and *Wealth* were written for the same variable theatre space as were the other plays of Aristophanes, with its dual focus of *orchestra* and flexible scenic façade. If the audience needed to employ a similar imagination as for Aristophanes' earlier plays in locating the central action, there was one major change. The chorus, whose nature dictated the original shape, had by the time of the last two plays dwindled in importance. For the forceful, anthropormorphic batches of wasps, birds or frogs, and the less fantastic but no less dominant conventions of men and women in various stages of grievance and frustration, *Women in Power* offers a chorus who function primarily as individuals, while in *Wealth* the Chorus retreat as the play progresses into virtual anonymity.

About 338 BC, fifty years after *Wealth* and twenty before the first Menander play, the Theatre of Dionysus was made permanent. This happened under the financial management of Lycurgus who extended the whole precinct and enlarged the auditorium. More significantly for the performance of plays, he had the *skene* built in stone, complete with a stage and side-wings to enclose the acting area. Whether this liberated stage design or restricted it is a moot point. Indications of location were still possible, by ornament or decoration, but the sheer solidity of a stone background is antipathetic to subtlety of reference. There is something daunting about the three storey stone Roman theatres which diminished all but the most spectacular action.

At the time of Lycurgus' changes to the structure of the theatre the programme of the festivals in Athens comprised in the main old tragedies and new comedies. The more popular tragedies were those which were more realistic and the new comedies tended to deal with everyday life. What is difficult to comprehend is why the physical structure should have become more substantial at the same time as the subject-matter was becoming less so. The background affects the performance. Aristophanes, even late Aristophanes, is written to be played frontally, acknowledging an audience at least seventy-five feet and, in the back rows, more like seventy-five yards away. Menander's use of direct address to the audience by his masked actors may point to a closer contact. The diminution of the chorus in Menander to the status of stage direction in the text could have been the result of this need to bring the action forward as far as possible, away from the *skene* and closer to the audience.

Such a development in the use of space still fails to account for the basic paradox. How should it happen that, at the very time when the themes of the drama retreat from epic to parish-pump, the building to house the new plays becomes literally fixed in stone? Menander, it is hard to doubt, would have benefited from more intimate stage conditions. The new and solider Theatre of Dionysus seems hardly the place for domestic comedy. The chorus, hitherto the drama's most spectacular effect, is on its last legs and will disappear altogether from the Roman adaptations. Late Aristophanes and any period Menander have no use for complex staging. Revelations and epiphanies are part of the past. Passion and angst make way for sunburn and backache.

This paradox has no obvious resolution except in so far as the theatre was as popular as ever, which may account for the fixing of its structure, while the licence which character-ised the heyday of Athenian supremacy seems to have succumbed to Athens' diminishing role as a political force. The contemporary satire which characterised Old Comedy was as unsophisticated as the system under which it flour-ished. The theatre's new concerns were dictated by audience taste but equally by political expediency. Many find this a decline, as the sentimental comedy of the eighteenth century cannot but appear small beer when compared with the raunchiness of the restoration repertoire. Fashions change though and the sentimental comedy was itself to spawn the sparkling comedies of manners of Sheridan and Goldsmith later the same century. As has always happened, the notable playwright is of his age but not bound by it. In this, Aristophanes was as typical and untypical of the comic writers of his time as have been Menander, Plautus and Terence, Moliere, Chekhov or Ayckbourn in theirs.

The basic situation of *Women in Power* is as inspired as any in the old comedies and it is set up in a scene which simultan-eously opens up a new comic vein and celebrates the theatre's love of itself. Plays like *Knights*, *Clouds* or *Wasps* had announced their central themes with disarming frankness: politics, education, lawcourts, all large targets waiting to be attacked. *Birds* and *Frogs* had more of a delayed action effect, starting off on one tack, disillusion with Athens or the need to resurrect a dead playwright, before taking off at a tangent to reveal a subtler message at crucial moments in the war. By the time of *Women in Power* the great war with Sparta is a thing of the past. So too is narrow political satire aimed at individuals and at their policies. Nothing, though, could be more broadly political than *Women in Power* which aims at the entire fabric of Athenian society, dominated as it was by forums of influence which were exclusively male.

These included the theatre, still a focus for ideas, albeit in emasculated form. The opening of *Women in Power* in such a context is inspired. Already in the *Lysistrata* of 411 BC. Aristophanes had suggested that women have a power to exercise, that of their sexuality. The withdrawing of favours until peace is engineered may have been an implausible ploy in a society which seemed to offer men so many outlets for sexual gratification other than their wives, but it is dramatically satisfying both in its simplicity and in its means of demonstration. Those means include the fact that all speaking roles in the Greek theatre were played by male actors. There are those who would argue that no women could appear on stage at all. The internal evidence of the plays is against this but the theatre, in all its essentials, was a male province, as were most aspects of public life at the time. *Lysistrata* is a rich parade of frustration, made all the more comic by the fact of the female characters being played by men in drag.

Women in Power extends the drag joke to its limits. The play opens with the arrival of first one woman, Praxagora, then the whole female chorus, wearing their husbands' clothes and disguised as men. They have decided that the only way to get any sense into politics is to hijack the Assembly and pass a motion bringing women into power. To do that they must pretend to be men in order to get a vote. So the audience has the prospect of a group of male actors, playing female characters who have disguised themselves as men in order to get women into power. This opening scene is extended to a quarter of the whole play.

Eventually the disguised women leave for the Assembly, to be replaced almost immediately by a couple of husbands, dressed up as women. The husbands have just woken up to find their own clothes missing and have been forced to put on their wives' clothes instead. This is the neatest of reversals, setting up a context of elaborate role-play which permeates all subsequent scenes. There is a theatrical logic to it that leads seamlessly into the outcome of the women's political success. For succeed, of course, they do and, after voting themselves into power, come up with a solution to society's ills which is as appropriate to the fourth century in its philosophy and execution as the sex-strike of *Lysistrata* was to the fifth.

Plato's *Republic* was not published until after Aristophanes' death but the ideas contained in that monumental discussion of the nature of justice and the nature of society were current in Athens and elsewhere from much earlier. Plato's mouthpiece is Socrates, put to death in 399 BC for promulgating precisely those ideas which made an unstable government feel most uncomfortable. Aristophanes must have known Socrates and the young Plato. He appears as a character in Plato's *Symposium*, one of the guests singing for their supper by offering individualistic opinions on the nature of love. Aristophanes' version of the history of the human race suggests that we were once double the size until split down the middle as a punishment: hence the constant search for our other half. The fable may be pure Plato but it has the ring of the dramatist alright.

Enjoying the hypothetical juggling with the social fabric that a drinking debate may turn up was not to prevent Aristophanes, given the chance, from sending up the philosophers. Political theory, he was well aware, is easier than political practice. Theories in Aristophanes have a habit of reaching logical conclusions. Once in power, the women of Aristophanes' play propose nothing more complex than *koinonia*, the concept of 'partnership' or 'community', with everyone giving and sharing in perfect harmony. At least, that is the idea until the problems created by human nature prove more intractable than those that their form of communism is set up to combat.

In *Birds* of 414 BC Aristophanes had taken on the idea of structuring a society from scratch. Cloudcuckooland, the city of the birds created half way between heaven and earth, is no Utopia and ultimately the play serves as a warning against allowing too much power to any individual. *Women in Power* remains firmly in Athens, an Athens whose political structure had notionally returned to the same as it was before defeat by the Spartans. But the handing over of power to the women results in an idealism which proves every bit as anarchic as did the experiment of Plato in practice when essayed by Hiero in Syracuse a few years later. The communist principle is undermined in part by human greed. It also falls foul of the sheer lack of will when aged crones – drag actors again – demand their sexual dues before the young man Epigenes can get round to the girl of his choice.

To suggest that *Women in Power* is the harbinger of a new form of comedy is neither to decry its inventiveness nor to suggest that it is markedly inferior to the plays of Aristophanes' early career. *Women in Power* and *Wealth* prove to be a less direct indication of how New Comedy will develop than Euripides' *Helen* or *Ion*. They do reflect a change in society and in society's expectations of the theatre. Maybe Aristophanes never expected to change the world. His early plays suggest he thought he could influence it. Experience proved him wrong but it is not maturity, still less cynicism, that points him in a new direction. The age of Athens as a single Hellenistic city in a world-wide, or at least eastern Europewide, culture may not have dawned but the sky on the horizon is rosy-fingered. To many, of course, this is the sunset and not the sunrise. Life in Athens was changing, that's for sure, and the last of the fifth century's playwrights was there to reflect it in the fourth.

Wealth opens in a simple enough but intriguing manner. A master and a slave enter in pursuit of a blind old man. The slave, Karion, complains to the audience about the way that his master Chremylos treats him and then demands to know why they are following the blind man. This is a standard exposition scene, loosely based on both double-act and master/servant relationship which, between them, will sustain two and a half thousand comedies in the next two and a half thousand years. It is not even original for Aristophanes. *Birds* opens with two Athenians, Euelpides and Peithetairos, on the trail of something about which the audience know nothing. The relationship between Dionysus and Xanthias at the opening of *Frogs* makes it clear that there is no novelty value in oppressive masters and oppressed slaves.

The blind man, it soon transpires, is the god Wealth, blinded by Zeus 'out of spite for mortals' (line 88), when he tried to bestow himself on decent people. Chremylos and Karion are on the way back from Delphi where Chremylos has been consulting the oracle to find out whether he should be advising his son to be honest in life, or dishonest, seeing as all the money ends up in the hands of the dishonest. Now having followed and unmasked the god of Wealth himself, he can provide an answer to his question as well as help the plot forward.

Chremylos' idea is to have Wealth cured of his blindness, as a result of which everyone who deserves money will be given it and everyone who doesn't will lose it. So far this is very much the world of Old Comedy with its lovely, simple solutions to nasty, intractable problems, of the kind which fantasy was created to sustain.

The arrival of the chorus is the first hint that here we have a development from the newer mood of *Women in Power* towards what might be termed comedy of reduced ambition. But if the target is less significant, the shots are still aimed at a real issue. The chorus do not put in their appearance until line 250. When they do arrive, they are elderly farmers. Not all of Aristophanes' early choruses are clouds, wasps or birds but they all have a role to play in helping, or sometimes hindering, the play's progress. The women of *Women in Power* function as characters in their own right. The farmers of *Wealth* have no real purpose. Simply friends of Chremylos, not very bright friends at that, they offer a dancing interlude.

For twenty-five lines they do a sheep and pig dance before subsiding into the role of passive bystanders. Apart from five minor interruptions, their further contribution is confined to half a dozen stage directions, *chorou*, suggesting that they sing a song or dance a dance, but that it is so marginally related to the plot, it is not worth recording in print. Menander's plays will take the tendency further with the identity of the chorus often as loose as 'a bunch of drunks' or 'some nasty-looking customers' whose approach the protagonists use as an excuse for leaving the stage.

The curious feature of *Wealth* is that it is possible to follow this change of dramatic direction almost while the playwright is writing. A later story suggests that our version was in part a rewrite of an earlier Old Comedy. *Wealth* certainly starts as Old Comedy but it ends up as New.

In his early plays Aristophanes makes constant use of contemporary reference. Current politicians, soldiers, philosophers, playwrights , many of them doubtless sitting in the audience, forced smiles on their faces, meet with scurrilous abuse. Euripides appears as a character in three separate plays and is good for a joke in the rest. Contemporary events are a source of satire but more, a source of serious comment on anything from the conduct of war to the handling of domestic affairs.

Direct comment is not wholly absent from *Wealth* but it has diminished to gums rather than teeth. None of the day's major issues gets an airing. There would be no way of telling, by reading *Wealth*, that Athens in 388 BC was once more engaged in hostilities with Sparta, if on a less cataclysmic scale than during the Peloponnesian War. The desire to speak in his own voice, latent in *Women in Power*, seems by *Wealth* to have passed Aristophanes by altogether. Digs at local celebrities are perfunctory, almost as though inserted against the playwright's better judgement. Such lip-service to audience expectation can still be found in Menander's *The Woman from Samos* where it rings true no more than in *Wealth*.

To this point *Wealth* would appear characterised exclusively by negative features, what it isn't rather than what it is.

There would be little point in promoting the play if it was no more than an example of Aristophanes when the juice had run dry. In reality *Wealth* continues the new direction begun in *Women in Power*, and takes it a stage further. The excision of public satire leaves room for a closer examination of private morality. The argument about the distribution of wealth is perennial and has ensured that this play survived when most of the rest of Aristophanes was consigned, if not to the scrap-heap, at least to the reserve shelves of the library.

Chremylos' initial dilemma over how to bring up his son seems solved by the decision to restore Wealth's sight. The entry of Poverty looking like 'the Demon Queen of some Greek tragedy', literally 'a Fury' (line 423), is more than a comic complication. Poverty's argument is a puritan one. 'I'm essential to human happiness', she suggests (line 469). 'If everyone was wealthy, who would work?' (line 510). She develops the argument ending on the note that gave the play its moral appeal when it returned to the schoolroom:

'Fear of me fills each working man's head

When he looks at his kids and his wife' (lines 532–3).

As a response to the emancipation of Wealth this cuts little ice. Chremylos does not want everyone rich, only those who deserve to be. It is still a serious, if hardly deep, appraisal of an approach to life which looks forward to Menander's realism.

Chremylos has the central task assigned to most of Aristophanes' leading Athenians of seeing off the opposition but the slave Karion shares the load. Karion has a scene with Chremylos' wife which has perplexed some critics, but the mistress/servant relationship is dramatically useful in providing an audience for Karion's narrative about the cure. More significantly, Chremylos' wife is the first female comic character in the drama whose personality is not fashioned by travesty. This is all the more apparent when her scene is sandwiched between those of Poverty and the Old Woman whose appearance and function depend largely on the maleness of the actor playing them. The Wife is not like this.

She may not have much more to do than act as a feed for Karion but the comic potential of the scene is not related to her sex. Hardly a blow for liberation the scene does herald a world in which relationships in and out of marriage may become the proper stuff of drama.

In *Wealth* a sense of character begins to dominate situation. The scenes with Hermes and the Secret Policeman have parallels in *Birds* but in *Wealth* they are less obvious. If the ending is predictable, the sheer good nature of the principals, Chremylos and Karion, ensures that the mood is always upbeat. The comparative absence of coarseness, combined with a humanist message, led to the recovery of the play when little else of Aristophanes was thought to merit translation. There was a performance in Greek in 1536 in St John's College, Cambridge, though this appears to have had more to do with a campaign for reformed pronunciation than any revivalist fervour. *Wealth* was the one Greek comedy to appear respectable when Plautus and Terence were enjoying a Latin revival. In 1652, during the interregnum when all the public theatres were closed, Thomas Randolph's adaptation received a private production under the wholly edifying title of *Hey for Honesty, Down with Knavery*. Even Addison found *Wealth* 'a very pretty allegory'. One small part of Aristophanes had become respectable. It took until the abolition of censorship in Britain in 1968 to liberate the rest.

The excitement which greeted the publication as late as 1959 of the first entire play of Menander to have survived, the *Duskolos*, here translated as *The Malcontent*, was matched by the disappointment of those who read it and discovered what they had been missing. Menander's reputation was of such a high order in the ancient world that it was assumed that, should a complete play ever turn up, we would be confronted with an obvious masterpiece, another *Twelfth Night* or *She Stoops to Conquer*, a play of wit and style, dealing with a world of society and sophistication. The major fragments known since the beginning of the century should have warned the overoptimistic that Menander's world is a confined one and one in which the sense of comedy is rooted less in situation than in character.

The patronising defence of *The Malcontent*, that it was probably early Menander, and hence atypical, has tended to mask the positive dramatic virtues of a play which turns out to be as effective in structure as it is acute in its observation of human behaviour.

It opens with a Prologue from the god Pan, whose shrine provides part of the setting, situated between the houses of Knemon, the malcontent of the title, and Gorgias, his stepson who left the house with his mother, Myrrhine, when Knemon's behaviour became intolerable. Knemon now lives with his daughter by Myrrhine and one old woman to look after him. A well-to-do young man called Sostratos has fallen in love with her but any attempts to get close enough to Knemon to seek his approval are met with a barrage of hostility and abuse.

Knemon is an obsessive, a misanthrope as antisocial as Molière's Alceste, though the lack of further parallels between the plays is enough to avoid Molière's title for the Menander. One thing, though, Knemon and Alceste do have in common. Their obsession is not without motive, justification even. Knemon lives in a world which is filled with the thoughtless and the bad-mannered, who trample across his land, expect to use his utensils as though they were their own or, in the case of Sostratos, marry his daughter simply because he fancies her. One of the most revealing moments in the play comes in Knemon's remarkable speech after being rescued from the well down which he has fallen (lines 708–747). 'Find her a husband', he tells Gorgias, his affable stepson, 'I couldn't do that even if I were in perfect health. Nobody would ever be good enough for her' (734–5).

This apparent recantation, the result of finding himself unable to cope without outside assistance, looks as though it will be the prelude to a standard happy ending. A lesser playwright would surely have created Knemon as a monster and redeemed him through Pauline conversion. Menander proves himself of subtler mind and more aware of what drives the solitary. Knemon's railing against the hypocrisy of those who believe their sacred feasts are for the gods has more than a shade of justice to it. His confession that he had lost his faith in human nature implies that he was not always as now. 'I'd watched how friendship had become no more than a commodity with a calculated profit margin' (719–20) is the response of a wry recluse rather than an embittered Timon.

Nor is this speech the end of the matter. Knemon's experience down the well may have chastened him. It has not changed him. If anything he threatens to become more of a hermit than before. The cruelty of his treatment at the hands of the slave, Getas, and the cook, Sikon, in the last act is barely offset by the clever transition into what is effectively the musical finale. Knemon ends up at the party after all. He is not a changed man, or not greatly, and the world about which he complained still contains, as Malvolio had cause to find out, a vicious streak in the hands of the natural persecutor.

Though the personality and treatment of the malcontent himself lie behind the actions of all the other characters in the play, Knemon's role is shorter than that of either Sostratos or Gorgias, and barely as long as that of the Cook, Sikon. Sostratos is a notional juvenile lead with the mixture of brainlessness and fecklessness that tends to characterise young men in classical comedy and hardly bodes well for his future wife. Fortunately, she is such a cipher she fails to merit as much as a name. One thing which is clear from reading both this play and *The Woman from Samos* is that Menander divides his characters into those who are worth bothering about and those who are not. Most of the women are as much stock characters by virtue of their gender as are the Cook or the Parasite from their professions. Potential relationships are scrupulously, perhaps ruthlessly, discarded in favour of the main concerns. None of the relationships between men and women has much substance.

The prologue does insist that this is a play about love. Love for Menander, it appears, is a man liking the look of a girl. The girl has little to say in the matter, except, on rare occasions, yes. Though much of the comedy of the seventeenth and eighteenth centuries is as one-sided, Menander does offer the prospect of a satisfactory union, a marriage fashioned, if not in heaven, at least at the instigation of a god. Knemon's daughter is regarded by Pan as 'our special care' because of her piety. He is happy to help the plot along if it means the girl leaving her father's house for the financial security of that of Sostratos. If your life is inevitably prescribed, it might as well be prescribed with money.

Gorgias is, apart from Knemon, the one character of depth. His basic good-heartedness makes his concern over his half-sister's welfare a serious matter. The pomposity with which he accosts Sostratos dissolves the moment he hears of Sostratos' good intentions. This apparent naivety has the edge of a countryman's cunning too as he gets a day's digging in the fields out of Sostratos who is labouring under the forlorn hope that Knemon is on his way to an adjoining patch. When he suggests the digging Gorgias has reason to expect that Knemon will turn up but he makes no attempt to make life easier for Sostratos.

In his own quiet way Gorgias has tried to keep open the last line of communication to Knemon and offer, if not an antidote to Knemon's misanthropy, at least an exception to his rule. The principals in Menander's plays may have decisive features but they are far from shallow. In *The Woman from Samos* we find a level of real complexity.

As soon as the scraps of Menander began to surface in the early years of this century, scholars and critics descended upon them like starving men at a banquet. Some of the fragments were reconstituted as whole plays. Gilbert Murray took the lead in this, publishing first *The Rape of the Locks*, based on *Perikeiromene*. Successful production inspired him to *The Arbitration* from the remains of *Epitrepontes*, a more difficult task because, though the play has more substance, the gaps are more substantial.

Should the whole of *Perikeiromene* or *Epitrepontes* ever turn up, posterity will be able to judge Murray's skill as seer and playwright. *The Woman from Samos*, surviving in little more than three hundred lines, was equally prone to attracting those who felt up to predicting the rest. The present translator has to confess to being one of their number, though less blatantly with eighty-five per cent of the text to work on. There may well be mistakes. One fragmentary reference to 'breaking a seal', around the missing line 30, is so obscure as to have defeated me entirely. A more enjoyable, if slightly malicious game, has been to compare the predictions of those who had only the three hundred lines available to them with the substantial portions of real Menander published only twenty years ago. One commentator thought that Chrysis had stolen Plangon's baby; another that Chrysis was the baby's mother with Demeas the father; a third was convinced that there were two babies all along. That noone guessed right is less a condemnation of their dramatic sense than a tribute to Menander's skill in keeping his audience guessing.

For the reader of the play in its present form, the cast-list and the status of the various relationships in *The Woman from Samos* may all seem rather predictable. Moschion has impregnated the girl next door while his father and hers are away on a business trip. Demeas is not Moschion's real father but adopted him as a baby in circumstances which are not clear. Though a bachelor, Demeas lives with a woman called Chrysis, the Samian of the play's title, who, being from Samos and not an Athenian, cannot legally marry him. The play opens with the return of the old men who have agreed between them that son and daughter should get married, for all that the neighbour, Nikeratos, is too poor to provide a dowry.

Then Demeas discovers a baby and the misunderstandings begin, leading to the concoction of eavesdroppings, dissemblings and explosions of unreason which contrived to defeat the unwary speculators of the early part of the century with no exposition scenes to guide them. On one subject only were these speculators in agreement. The play must end with Chrysis turning out to be a free woman after all, perhaps the long-lost daughter of Nikeratos, so that Demeas can end up marrying her. This, we now know, never happens, unless a lost Epilogue turns up to satisfy the romantics at an off-stage stroke. Apart from a non-speaking entry with the bride, Plangon, at the wedding celebrations, the title character has no role to play in the last act.

A modern audience may want the conclusion of a well-made play with all the ends tied up. *The Woman from Samos* and *The Malcontent* suggest that this is not part of the Menander method. To expect it is to overlook Menander's intentions and to romanticise his plays beyond the necessary 'happy ending'. There is a realism to Menander which brings to life the people of his time as do no plays from the fifth century BC. Humans are sufficiently complex not to change their natures as they might their clothes. They react instinctively to new circumstance and to new information. Only after the heat of the moment do they give consideration to these new circumstances and modify, perhaps, their position. The main characters learn from experience. *The Woman from Samos* is built on a pattern of revised positions. At base this is no more than a manipulation of the Aristotelian principles of *peripeteia* and *anagnorisis*, 'reversal' and 'recognition', but Menander reaches a level of complexity unrivalled until Shakespeare.

By proposing a resolution of Chrysis' social position, those early critics made the assumption that a play to which she gives the title ought to focus as much on her as on the other central characters. The reader may in all humanity want to see her recompensed for the way in which she is treated by Demeas and then by Nikeratos. The fact remains that, fully developed as she may be within the range of options open to her, Chrysis is less a protagonist than a catalyst.

Chrysis is in an invidious, though not unfamiliar, position in Menander's world. Preserved from the life of a common courtesan, which was the most she could hope for as a foreigner in Athens, her domestic position is that of mistress or, effectively, whatever Demeas cares to make it. He claims to be in love with her but was only persuaded to offer her the protection of his roof, in order to keep possible rivals at bay. His command to her not to have a child because it could only be a bastard evokes neither surprise nor revulsion in the rest of the household. Unsavoury as all this seems today, the comedy's serious aspect does not benefit from playing down the casual cruelty. When Demeas discovers that she does apparently have a child and that Moschion seems to be the father, he places all the blame on her:

> 'The woman's a whore, an infection. Well, what of it? She won't get round me. Be a man, Demeas. Govern your passions. Fall out of love' (lines 348–50).

Such a reaction might be put down to a supposed cuckold's pain but the same defence can hardly be offered in the scene where he turns her out of the house:

> 'Something special, are you? You'll soon find out how you rate in the city. Ten drachmas a go and a free dinner. Till you die of drink. If you don't like the idea of that, then starve' (lines 390–5).

This is a world where women are objects. What saves the play, I hope, from a sourness that no modern palate could tolerate is what Chrysis manages to make of her position. Her sheer common sense is on a different plane from that of any of the men. This is something that they all recognise and part of what has inspired Demeas' passion for her which, in spite of everything, looks remarkably close to love. Chrysis knows that under normal circumstances she is far from a doormat. Had her own child lived, she would have found a way to keep it and to win Demeas round. This is why she is so shocked by her rejection: as, indeed, is Nikeratos who takes her in, until he comes to believe she has been cooking up a conspiracy against him.

Menander pulls no punches in the scene between Demeas and Chrysis as the above sample of dialogue bears witness. Both characters are suffering and Demeas can lash out only because he has the authority to do so. What preserves the scene from being too vicious for any comedy is that there is a third party present, the Cook, whose comic presence and occasional interventions go a long way to disarming Demeas' anger and preserving him from becoming wholly unsympathetic.

Behind all of Menander is a seriousness about human relationships that only strong feelings, strongly expressed, can advance. But of all the relationships in the play, only one seems really important to him, that between father and son. For all that Chrysis performs all the functions of a wife and, indeed, mother in Demeas' household, her intervention in the last act would be a distraction. Demeas is not Moschion's natural father. This has made him the more prone to spoiling him. Nikeratos, Myrrhine, the slave Paphlagon and Chrysis, all feed this basic examination, creating a context in which to test father and son.

Demeas is a mixture of affable and irritable, a man convinced of his self-control. His previous reluctance to invite Chrysis into his home is a prelude to his refusing to explain why he wants her out again. Moschion is equally consistent, embarrassed to spell out his misdemeanours to the audience and as adept as his father at failing to communicate. The final scene is the key to their relationship with Moschion's bluff prevailing but only through Demeas' basic goodwill. Demeas' apology: 'Oh Moschion. You're upset and I love you for it' (lines 694–714), is a speech of real feeling, tinged with reproof.

The Woman from Samos combines sentiment and savagery, but it treats people as creatures of both affection and passion. Within a social framework which today must seem as unfair as it is inflexible, there is room to recognise domestic problems for their broad application. This above all ensured that the playwrights of Rome returned so often to Greek New Comedy as the source of their own material. It ensured too that this new seam, of which recognisable human behaviour was the core, would fuel an entire European tradition and end up, tired but not yet exhausted, daily on the small screens of our living-rooms.

J Michael Walton

ARISTOPHANES: OLD AND NEW

'Old' comedy and the late plays

Evidence suggests that it is harder for writers to keep up a consistent standard in comedy than in tragedy. Few comedy playwrights in history have equalled the numbers of plays written by Aeschylus, Sophocles and Euripides, and those who have – Goldoni and Labiche spring to mind – show wild fluctuations in level, style and funniness. (It would be interesting, in this context as in almost every other, to have sight of Menander's whole output, over 100 plays.) Even forty comedies (Aristophanes' total) is a large number: as many as Molière, more than Plautus or Feydeau or Holberg wrote, many times more than Terence or Wilde or Coward. Performers of comedy, too, often have a short shelf-life: most comedians have done their best or most characteristic work by their fifties, and thereafter tend either to repeat themselves or to branch out in new (and not always successful) ways. (The great creative film comedians of this century, Chaplin, Keaton, Laurel and Hardy, Lloyd, Tati, are notable examples.) Only a few comic creators – P.G. Wodehouse is an egregious 20th-century instance – continue into extreme old age the style and freshness they first achieved in youth.

Michael Walton, in his part of the Introduction to this volume, has suggested plausible external reasons – political and social – why Aristophanes may have changed his style after 405BC, why indeed no stage comedy was ever the same again. (Such pressures are a far more likely explanation than those offered by desk-bound, text-bound scholars of earlier generations, who claimed, amazingly, that Aristophanes' change of style was the result of a stroke, or even that the late plays are by someone else.) I believe that the 'new' direction in his work is the result not only of external forces, but came also from within; that the changes we see in the last two surviving plays are part of a continuous process of creative evolution; that Aristophanes' surviving plays show an organic development throughout his career, a development paralleled in the surviving work of no other ancient playwright.

At first glance, one tends to notice differences rather than similarities between the plays written before and after 405BC. In the two surviving late plays Aristophanes uses the Chorus less often, and more perfunctorily, than in earlier work. He makes fewer political and topical allusions. The central issues of his plots are more general and more 'philosophical' – one might almost say more cerebral. His characters are, by and large, less fantastical, rooted in everyday reality rather than in fantasy. His verse is less showy, and there is far less lyricism. Other elements remain unchanged: his farcical invention is just as wild, his satire (for all that its butts are now domestic instead of public) is just as scabrous, his sexual and scatological humour is more exuberant than ever. But the differences seem to outweigh such similarities, as if Aristophanes had indeed made a conscious and calculated change in artistic direction after 30 highly successful years in the business.

This impression is illusion. All apparent changes in the late plays are actually the culmination of ideas already present, in one form or another, in Aristophanes' work from the very start. The role of the Chorus is a clear example. In plays up to and including *Birds* (414BC) the Chorus seems to conform to a 'traditional' pattern: it is integral to the action, bristles with 'attitude' and has a stake in the outcome of the dilemma which underlies the plot. But even as early as *Clouds* (423BC) and *Peace* (421BC) Aristophanes was also placing some chorus-utterances laterally to the action, using them to create atmosphere and to provide what in modern ballet are called *divertissements*: technical displays meant to be enjoyed for their own sake and largely irrelevant to the main matter of the plot. In *Frogs* this function is crucial to the other-worldly feeling of the action; the *divertissements* are integral; the Frogs and Initiates, whose words at first glance seem self-referential and irrelevant, are in fact the heart of the play. In *Lysistrata* and *Festival Time* (*Thesmophoriazousai*) Aristophanes splits his Chorus into groups, and gives some 'traditional' Chorus material to single characters – the opening and closing scenes in Lysistrata and the trial scene, unmasking scene and rescue scenes in *Festival Time* are examples. It is a short, and entirely logical, step from such changes to the virtual replacement of the Chorus in *Women in Power* (*Ekklesiazousai*) by single characters (the women at the beginning, the Town Crieress at the end), and by its almost wholly celebratory and *divertissement* role in Wealth.

In the same way, changes in the role of the comic protagonist, apparently such a feature of the two late plays, are no new thing at all. Aristophanes had been experimenting for years with different ways of articulating comic initiative between the actors, and of giving his plot momentum through individual characterisation and group interaction. *Acharnians* and *Peace* (and in a different way, *Birds*) are the only plays centring on single, pivotal figures. *Knights* and *Wasps* hinge on comic contests, in which the two participants have equal weight. *Festival Time* centres on a double-act (Mnesilochos and Euripides); *Frogs* gives comic initiative to all three actors. The main character in *Lysistrata* is serious throughout, and comic initiative comes from others (Myrrhine, the Spartan, the Athenian); the play also shares dominance, scene by scene, among different characters, so that even a cameo doorkeeper gets to lead a scene. There is therefore nothing new about the way Praxagora drops out of dominance in *Women in Power* (surrendering the initiative to Blepyros, the Hags and the Town Crieress), or the way Chremylos and Karion alternate, in *Wealth*, as comic protagonists. Novelty (for us, at least, who know only these two of Aristophanes' later plays) consists less in such apparent divergences from 'Old Comedy' style than in the way they are mingled with elements which seem wholly (and some would say, gloriously) traditional, for example the Informer scene in *Wealth* or the dance which closes *Women in Power*.

The late plays and 'New' comedy
So far as later comedy, from New Comedy onwards, is

concerned, two developments in Aristophanes' later plays are of particular significance. First is the way in which he handles the *alazon* tradition. The *alazon* ('sponger') is one of the earliest components of comedy: a buffoon outsider who tries to disrupt the plot, sets out to spoil things for the protagonist, and is discomforted and driven out. In Aristophanes' earlier plays *alazones* are of all kinds: informers, oracle-mongers, braggart soldiers, bread-women, inept poets, bullies, thieves and drunks. Their scenes are usually short (sometimes only a single joke), and are the occasion for parody (usually of poetry or professional ritual), slapstick or both at once. Often the *alazon* is a dialect part, or has some mockable physical peculiarity. We are, in short, in the territory later to be occupied by the eccentric dancers, drunks and braggarts of 20th-century music-hall. Aristophanes' *alazon*-play *par excellence* is *Birds*, in which no less than fourteen such characters appear, perform their party pieces and are sent packing. But even from the start of his career, he experimented with a dozen ways of integrating the *alazones* with the plot. In *Wasps* they become the defendant, accuser and witnesses in a mock trial, the assault-victims and torch-girl Philokleon picks up on a drunken spree, and the three crab-dancers who lead the final spectacle. All are controlled by the dominant metaphor of the plot; all advance, rather than interrupt, the action. In *Frogs* the *alazon* tradition is worked up into the beating-scene, the scenes with the Corpse and the Landlady, even Empousa's brief appearance – and Aristophanes' shifting of comic initiative allows him to give *alazon* characteristics to any of his main characters at will, until the weighing-scene (*alazon*-business *in excelsis*) crowns the comic action. In *Lysistrata alazon*es are again integral: Myrrhine and Kinesias, the Athenian Commissioner, the Spartan delegation, the drunks in the second half. In *Festival Time* the *alazon*-tradition takes over the whole second half: Euripides' rescue-attempts, and the reactions of the dialect Policeman, the deadpan Woman and above all of Mnesilochos himself, the *alazon* promoted to leading character.

This development continues in the two late plays. The only truly 'traditional' *alazon* scene is that with the Secret Policeman and Honest Citizen in *Wealth* – and however well its theme is integrated with that of the plot, the scene still seems somewhat schematic, plastered on the play rather than organic to it. More characteristic are the Poverty and Hermes scenes in *Wealth* and the Blepyros/Chremes scene in *Women in Power*. These have 'traditional' *alazon*-scene characteristics (self-contained silliness, cockiness and the feeling that gags rather than dramatic dialogue are being performed), but they also show a depth of character quite unlike that in earlier plays – comparison of the part of Hermes in *Wealth* and in *Peace* is enough to make the point. The Blepyros/Chremes scene in particular, although it is – as Michael Walton has pointed out – the forerunner of hundreds of such scenes in later comedies, is like nothing else in extant Aristophanes. We are invited to laugh not merely at the situation, but at the characters as shown in the situation and at the way they reveal their character as the scene progresses. The apotheoses of the *alazon* tradition – and by any standards, among the finest pieces of knockabout Aristophanes ever wrote – are the Hags scene in *Women in Power* and the Old Woman/Young Man scene in *Wealth*. In each case – this may be just coincidence, the fact that only these texts survive – the main characters are played by men in drag, great-great-grandparents of every *commedia dell'arte* Bawd or pantomime Ugly Sister since. The humour depends on our awareness that the grotesque 'women' are caricatures played by men; if there were the slightest illusion of real femininity (as there can be, for example, in the performance of Myrrhine or Praxagora), the scenes would collapse in distastefulness and cruelty. Even so, Aristophanes gives these old women more character than any other of his travesty parts: pathos underlies the hilarity, the grotesqueness is pitiful as well as wished-for, in a way more common in later comedy than in any of his earlier work. The relationship between the Old Woman and Young Man in *Wealth*, in particular, has a ring of verisimilitude, of ordinary (if heightened) real life, which ambushes and all but confounds the slapstick.

The second major development in the late plays, a precursor of subsequent dramatic practice, is in character-drawing. In all Aristophanes' earlier plays – and, it is fair to add, in all extant Greek tragedy – character is applied, so to speak, from outside the role. The people have no personality outside the situation: they are defined not by who they are, but by their role in the story. Electra, Medea, Philoctetes, Agamemnon – however grand they are and however much their plight arouses compassion and terror – all remain lay-figures, myth-inspired outlines despite the bright colouring-in provided by the dramatist. Something similar is true of most characters in Aristophanes. Dikaiopolis, Agorakritos, Trygaios, Strepsiades, Lysistrata – all derive character from their situation: first in relation to the dilemma which opens the play, and then from what happens when they set out to solve it. They are Jonsonian humours rather than characters in any modern sense. Others – Dionysos in *Frogs*, Euripides in *Festival Time*, not to mention such lesser figures as Hermes in *Peace*, Euripides and Aeschylus in *Frogs*, Euelpides in *Birds* – have their character determined before the action begins, and neither deviate from it nor develop it (as Peithetairos does in *Birds*, say, or Mnesilochos in *Festival Time*). However dazzling or fascinating they seem, they are two-dimensional throughout; we are in the world not of dramatic characteris-ation (at least as later generations have understood it), but of sitcom or music-hall.

In the late plays, characterisation is of an entirely different order. The women who open *Women in Power* may seem individually characterless, but together (and despite comic exaggeration) they form a recognisable, human and above all 'female' group. Blepyros, Pheidolos and Chremes seem less like figures in farce than like ordinary citizens who happen to have strayed onstage. This is even more the case with Chremylos and Karion in *Wealth* – and their ordinari-ness is brilliantly exploited in their scene with Poverty, a melodramatic lay-figure from whom they seem to inhabit an entirely different world. The pretty girl who fancies Epigenes in *Women in Power*, and Chremylos' Wife in *Wealth*, show flashes of individuality which have nothing to do with the situation of their scenes. They are characterised from within, and seem, as people in real life do, to be withholding as much of themselves as they choose to reveal. We feel that we know all there is to know about even as protean a figure as Philokleon; with the characters in *Women in Power* and *Wealth*, we feel that their lives could continue, in unforesee-able ways, once the play is done.

High comedy and low

In the light of later trends in comedy, from New Comedy onwards, these developments in Aristophanes' late plays are fascinating. We may regret that none of his other late work survives, or that he died before he could further explore such exciting territory. But the developments also have their dark side. The growth of the comic tradition, from Menander onwards, gradually led to a split between comedy of charac-ter and comedy of situation. Character comedy became the norm in 'literary' circles, and has attracted most of the (very sparse) critical writing about stage comedy. Scholars even presumed to call it 'high comedy', as if the fact that they gave it their attention were enough, alone, to lift it to the heights. 'Low comedy' became the province of performers, and its skills – *lazzi* (physical routines such as those of the *commedia dell'arte* or circus clowning), dialect comedy, 'acts' of every kind – were dismissed by the high-falutin' as vulgar and irrelevant to the 'artistic' mainstream. (Even today, few 'high' comic actors can juggle, or roller-skate, or fall, as Chaplin or Keaton did. Few 'high' comic writers regard such business as integral to comedy, or incorporate it in their scripts. Few dons pay any attention at all to 'low' performers in their exegeses of comedy.) That such distinctions are nonsense, that comedy can be a single, indivisible art, is the true main message of all Aristophanes' work. His later plays belong to the same tradition as his earlier plays, and if we in the West have lost sight of that tradition, if we are only just rediscovering it (in the work of such people as Dario Fo, Steve Martin or Théâtre de Complicité), then the loss has been ours from first to last.

Kenneth McLeish

Note: line-numbers alongside the texts relate to the Greek original rather than to the translation.

ARISTOPHANES

WOMEN IN POWER
(Ekklesiazousai, 'Assemblywomen')

translated by Kenneth McLeish

Characters

PRAXAGORA *Sofia*
FIRST WOMAN *Anita*
SECOND WOMAN *Ida*
THIRD WOMAN *Lara W.*
BLEPYROS *Bruce*
PHEIDOLOS *Scott*
CHREMES *Martin*
TOWN CRIERESS *Cristina.*
PRETTY GIRL *Sarah*
EPIGENES *Johnathan.*
FIRST HAG *Amanda.*
SECOND HAG *Angel.*
THIRD HAG *Catherine.*

SLAVE (silent part)

CHORUS of WOMEN *Christina.*
Amanda
Angel.

A street in Athens. Night. Enter PRAXAGORA, *disguised as a man, and carrying a lamp which she places on a pedestal and addresses with reverence.*

PRAXAGORA.

    O eye! Bright eye! O second Sun!
    O triumph of the potter's art,
    O lamp, O monster born of clay
    Whose nostrils breathe the Sun's own fire,
    Be our beacon, our messenger, today.
    We trust no one else. Only to you
    Do we bare ourselves; only you
    Are allowed to watch the games we play:
    Love games, sweet wrestling in the night.   10
    You watch, and no one puts you out.
    You know our secret places, singe
    The thickets between our thighs; you come
    Down to the cellar where the wine is stored,
    A silent friend who never tells.
    And now, you can share our secret plans
    For this Assembly, where we, today –

    Oh, it's too bad! Where are they? It'll soon
    Be dawn. The Assembly starts at first light.   20
    They said they'd be here. We ought to be ready,
    In our places. 'Be prepared', as someone said.
    What's happened to hold them up? Is it their
        beards?
    Or was it too hard to steal their husband's clothes?
    Ah . . . there's a light.
    Who's coming? I'd better get out of the way.
    It might be a *man* . . . and that would never do.

    Enter some WOMEN, *dressed in men's clothes.*

FIRST WOMAN.

    This way, chaps. Pick up your feet, come on.   30
    The cock crowed, y'know, just as we started out.

PRAXAGORA.

    Thank goodness you're here. I've been up all night.

I'll just see if my next-door neighbour's ready.
The tiniest tap . . . we don't want her husband
To hear . . .

She taps on a house-door. The SECOND WOMAN
comes out.

SECOND WOMAN.
Shh! It's all right. I heard you.
I was just trying to get these shoes on . . .
My husband . . . you've no *idea* what it's like.
He's a fisherman – and when we get to bed
He just wants to row all night.
40 I just *couldn't* get his clothes until now.

FIRST WOMAN.
Oh, look: down the road. Here come the others.

Enter more WOMEN, *all dressed as men.*

SECOND WOMAN.
Oh, do be quick! Don't you remember
What Glyke said? The last one here
Was to pay for the cakes, and *all* the drinks . . .

FIRST WOMAN.
Who's that, trying to run in those boots?
Oh, it's Smikythion's wife.

SECOND WOMAN.
Must be. He always did like a loose fit.

FIRST WOMAN.
Isn't that the innkeeper's wife?
50 Look: the one with the enormous torch.

SECOND WOMAN.
They're all coming. Every woman in Athens . . .

THIRD WOMAN (*as she enters*).
Praxagora, darling! You've simply no *idea*
How hard it was to slip away. My husband
Was at it the whole night long. Red in the face.
He *always* burps when he eats sardines.

PRAXAGORA.
    I think we're all here. Gather round. Sit down.
    Now, have you all done what we arranged to do?

FIRST WOMAN.
    Oh yes. I haven't shaved under my arms   60
    For *weeks*, just like we said. It's like a *wood*
    Under there. And every day, when my husband
    Goes out to work, I oil myself all over
    And sit in the sun, to get a manly tan.

SECOND WOMAN.
    Me too. I threw my razor out at once.
    You should *see* the undergrowth. I don't
    Look like a woman down there at all.

PRAXAGORA.
    Have you all got your beards, as we agreed?

FIRST WOMAN.
    Heavens, yes. What about this one, then?

SECOND WOMAN.
    What about this one? Isn't he lovely?   70

PRAXAGORA.
    What about the others?

FIRST WOMAN.
    Yes, they're nodding. They've got theirs.

PRAXAGORA.
    I can see you've everything else you need.
    Men's clothes, and proper cloaks, and walking
        sticks.

FIRST WOMAN.
    I got this from my husband when he was still asleep.

SECOND WOMAN.
    Is *that* your husband's? How *does* he get it up?

FIRST WOMAN.
    Practice. He's been doing it for years. You know
        him: 80
    Picks up anything that's not tied down.

PRAXAGORA.
> Ladies . . . ladies . . . we've got to make our plans
> Now, before the stars go in. The Assembly
> Begins at dawn: we've got to be ready.

FIRST WOMAN.
> We'll have to get the places at the front,
> On the rows just before the speaker's stand.

THIRD WOMAN.
> I've brought *this*. I don't care *how* boring it is.

PRAXAGORA.
> How *boring* . . . ?

THIRD WOMAN.
90
> Yes, darling. The men, you know. Arguing.
> I can work away as I listen. I mean,
> My little ones . . . they haven't a *stitch* to wear.

PRAXAGORA.
> Oh, yes. Oh, very nice. One look at you,
> They'll know you're a man, all right. Put it away!
> Now then, make sure your cloaks are properly on.
> It would be dreadful if we got there late,
> When the whole place was full, and had to climb
> Over the benches to find a seat. Suppose
> One of us tripped, and her cloak slipped,
> And everyone saw . . . ? If we get there first
> We can sit down and arrange ourselves in peace.
100
> Once you're comfortable, fasten on your beards.
> If we're wearing beards, they're sure to think
>   we're men.

SECOND WOMAN.
> She's right. Remember that pansy Agyrrios?
> He grew a beard, everyone took him for a man,
> And he went all the way in politics.

PRAXAGORA.
> Exactly.
> And that's what *we're* going to do today.
> We're going to stand up, take over the state,

And run it like it's never been run before.
Women in power! We can't do worse than men.

FIRST WOMAN.
There's just one problem. Women in power . . .   110
We've no experience.

PRAXAGORA.
Of course we have.
Just look at the young *men* in power today.
How d'you think *they* learned to argue, and talk
Till they had it the way they wanted it?
By lying down and taking it in bed, of course.
We're naturally equipped.

FIRST WOMAN.
Yes, but that's not . . . *public* experience.

PRAXAGORA.
Well, isn't that exactly why we're here?
To practise what we're going to say, before
The Assembly starts? Quick, on with your beards –
Yes, all of you, however good you are.

FIRST WOMAN.
Oh, we're all *good* at it! Talking, I mean . . .   120

PRAXAGORA.
Put on your beards, then. Turn into men.
Here are the wreaths . . . proper speaker's wreaths
Like they use in the Assembly. I'll wear this one:
I may just want to make a speech myself.

THIRD WOMAN.
Oh, darling, look! It's too ridiculous.

PRAXAGORA.
What is?

THIRD WOMAN.
What *do* we look like? Hairy mops.

PRAXAGORA.
Pray silence. Let the padre come forward.
Bring in the sacrificial pussy.

FIRST WOMAN.
You mean pig, surely?

PRAXAGORA.
We'll practise on the cat.
Put it down there. Oh, do stop chattering!
130   Now then, who wishes to address us first?

THIRD WOMAN.
Oh, me please!

PRAXAGORA (*handing her the speaker's wreath*).
Come forward, then. Speak in good health.

Pause. The THIRD WOMAN *seems to be waiting.*

THIRD WOMAN (*at last*).
Well yes . . . I'd simply *love* one.

PRAXAGORA.
One what?

THIRD WOMAN.
A drink, darling. You did say 'Good health'.

PRAXAGORA (*taking the wreath*).
Really! You've no idea at all of politics.

THIRD WOMAN.
You mean . . . politicians don't even *drink*?

PRAXAGORA.
Oh, do sit down.

THIRD WOMAN.
No, I mean they *must* drink.
Look at the laws they pass.

SECOND WOMAN.
140   It's all *parties*, too.
How can they have parties, if they never drink?

THIRD WOMAN.
All that shouting and fighting. They *must* drink.

PRAXAGORA.
Will you sit down, and stop wasting time?

THIRD WOMAN.
   I never asked for a beard in the first place.
   It tickles . . . and it makes my throat so dry . . .

PRAXAGORA.
   Does anyone else want to speak?

FIRST WOMAN.
   Yes. I do.

PRAXAGORA (*giving her the wreath*).
   Come forward, then. Perhaps we'll get
      somewhere now.
   Speak up, like a man. That's right: lean on your
      stick.   150

FIRST WOMAN.
   Unaccustomed as I am, I'd have liked
   To yield the floor to a better man than me,
   And learn from his experience. But still . . .
   I'll give my vote to any motion about *bars*:
   What we want is far less water in the wine.
   I mean, my goodness me, it's *dreadful* how . . .

PRAXAGORA.
   'My goodness me'? 'It's dreadful'? Oh, sit down.

FIRST WOMAN.
   What's wrong? *She* asked for a drink, not me.

PRAXAGORA.
   No, no, no. What man ever says 'My goodness',
   Or 'It's dreadful'? Everything else was fine.

FIRST WOMAN.
   Ah.

   (*as a man*)

   By gad, sir, somethin' must be done . . .

PRAXAGORA.
   Do stop.   160
   We've got to get it right, every detail,
   Or there's no point going on with it at all.

THIRD WOMAN.
No, no, let me try. I've *got* to try again.
I've thought it out . . . I'll get it right this time.

(*as a man*)

The whole point of the thing is this, ladies . . .

PRAXAGORA.
Ladies? You'd stand up there and call them ladies?

THIRD WOMAN.
Well, you know, with some it's rather hard to tell.

PRAXAGORA (*taking the wreath*).
Do be quiet. Go and sit over there.
170 I'm going to speak.
God guide our words today.

My friends, we're all citizens: we take part
In the state, and its troubles affect us all.
I can see how it's going downhill; I can see
How things keep getting worse and worse.
Must I suffer in silence? Must I put up with it?
Look at out leaders: they're all fools or crooks.
They spend one day helping the state, and ten
Helping themselves. If you get rid of one lot,
The next are worse. And it's all your fault, you
      know.
180 You never listen; you adore bad advice.
If a man's on your side you throw him out;
If he's not, you crawl to him and give him power.
In the old days, we didn't need an Assembly
To decide who was corrupt and who was loyal –
But now? Now everyone's in politics;
Everyone takes a hand. Something for nothing:
If a man offers that, we vote for him;
If not, we call him a crook and throw him out.

SECOND WOMAN.
That was lovely, dear. She's awfully good.

FIRST WOMAN.
190 'Awfully good'? Don't you know anything?

Suppose you come out with 'awfully good' in *there*?

SECOND WOMAN.
Oh, but I'd never say it *there*.

FIRST WOMAN.
Well then,
Don't keep saying it here.

SECOND WOMAN.
Shh! She's off again.

PRAXAGORA.
Things have simply never been so chaotic.
Look at the alliance we made with Thebes
Against the Spartans. When it was up
For approval, we said it was the only way
To save the state; as soon as it was made
The proposer of the bill had to run
For his life. The ship-building programme:
If you're poor and you want a job, you vote yes;
If you're rich and pay ship-tax, you vote no;
If you're a farmer . . . you vote no anyway.
Nothing stays the same for two days on end.
One minute you hate the Corinthians
And they hate you; next minute they're allies,
And you're busting a gut to be nice to them.   200
You think fools are brilliant, brilliant men are fools.
Quick! Wasn't that a *policy* just now?
Too late, it's gone: we threw the proposer out.

SECOND WOMAN (*as a man*).
The fellow's talking sense.

(*in a normal voice*)

How was that?

FIRST WOMAN.
Just right.

PRAXAGORA.
People of Athens . . . *gentlemen* . . . it's all your fault.
You all talk grandly about 'our common aim',

But when you come down to it, it's each man for
    himself.
What's the answer, did you say? I'll tell you:
210   Women. We must hand over the affairs of state
To women. They run the home; let them run the state.

CHORUS.
Hear, hear! Yes, yes! Hurray! Go on! More, more!

PRAXAGORA.
Women are better than men. I'll give you
Examples to prove it. Here's one: every day
They wet their wool the *usual* way –
No new-fangled methods. And what do we do,
We men in the Assembly? We're *always*
220   Experimenting, always playing about.

When they bake, they *squat*, like mother did;
They carry a *pot*, like mother did;
They have holy *days*, like mother did,
And funny *ways*, like mother did;
They henpeck us and wear us away
Like mother did;
They have lovers in day after day
Like mother did;
They adore honey-bread,
And drinking, and *bed* –
Oh, most of all, bed! –
Just like mother did.

230   So, gentlemen, there's nothing to discuss,
No need to ask what their policies are.
We should let them get started right away,
Put the state in their hands and let them rule.
You *know* it makes sense. Take the army first:
Each soldier has a Mum, who loves her son,
Looks after him, and sends his favourite food.
Financing expeditions? No problem:
They're not like us, you know: easy come, easy go –
They've been used to getting what they want, from
    birth.

What more need I say? Vote for my motion now,
And kiss hard lives goodbye – for evermore! 240

FIRST WOMAN.
Brilliant!

SECOND WOMAN.
Superb!

THIRD WOMAN.
Praxagora, *darling*!
Where did you learn to speak like that?

PRAXAGORA.
Oh, during the Troubles my husband and I
Lived over there, behind the Assembly-place.
I listened to the speakers then, and learned.

SECOND WOMAN.
No wonder you're so good at politics.
If your plan works, and we get power today,
We'll elect you our leader on the spot.

FIRST WOMAN.
But what about Kephalos? If he stands up
And starts insulting you, what will you do?

PRAXAGORA.
The potter? I'll say he's mad.

FIRST WOMAN.
They know that already. 250

PRAXAGORA.
Depressive mania.

FIRST WOMAN.
They know that, too.

PRAXAGORA.
All right, I'll ask them if they'll really let
A man so . . . *potty* . . . run the state to . . . *pot*.

FIRST WOMAN.
What if Neokleides rolls his eye at you?

PRAXAGORA.
I'll tell him to roll it . . . up a dog's behind.

SECOND WOMAN.
　But suppose they start knocking you?

PRAXAGORA.
　Knocking?
　I know about knocking. I'll see to them.

THIRD WOMAN.
　Suppose those big . . . tough . . . *brutal* policemen
　Come and grab you . . . and *squeeze* you . . . ?

PRAXAGORA.
　I'll squeeze *them*.
260　Make their eyes water. That'll deal with them.

SECOND WOMAN.
　And we can help! We can do our bit!

FIRST WOMAN.
　But there's another thing. How do we vote
　When the motion's called? With our arms like
　　this . . .
　Or this . . . ? I've never done it like a man.

PRAXAGORA.
　It *is* a problem. We'd better practise now.
　Take the *right* sleeve in the *left* hand, and pull
　It back. Then hold out the bare arm . . . That's it.
　Now then, hitch up your dresses, out of sight.
270　Boots on. Come on, you've all seen your husbands
　Getting ready to go out. Now, the beards . . .
　Make sure they're straight. Cloaks next. You've all
　Managed to get one? Good. Pull them right round.
　Now, lean on your walking sticks, like a choir
　Of greybeards singing the good old songs.
　They'll think we're farmers, in town for the day.

THIRD WOMAN.
　Lovely!

SECOND WOMAN.
　Come on. Let's go in front.

FIRST WOMAN.
　There *are*

Some ladies coming from the country. They said
They'd go straight to the Assembly, and meet us
  there.

PRAXAGORA.
  Is everyone ready? Come on, then.   280
  You know the rule: the Assembly starts at dawn,
  And if you're late, no pay. Not one bent pin.

FIRST WOMAN.
  All right, *men*. Let's be on our way.
  Remember you're men, all through today.
  Do nothing odd, cause no surprise.
  We'll win the prize; we'll show those guys.

CHORUS.
  Come on! Look sharp! Be quick!

SECOND WOMAN.
  In the middle of the night
  Long before the morning light
  Get up, get dressed, let's go.   290
  If we're not there at the start
  They won't let us play our part,
  And we want to steal the show.

THIRD WOMAN.
  Get inside and find a place.
  Folded arms and frowning face.
  Fight hard! Support the cause.
  When our leader states her plan –
  No, *his*, now she's a man –
  Give her cheers and loud applause.

CHORUS.
  Come on! Be quick! Look sharp!

FIRST WOMAN.
  Push the others aside.
  Get the best seats inside.
  Don't hesitate or cower.   300
  This Assembly doesn't need
  Men's laziness and greed:

It needs *us* – women in power.

SECOND WOMAN.
The old-timers were proud,
A self-disciplined crowd
(Each brought his own packed lunch);

THIRD WOMAN.
They were manly and firm,
Didn't fidget and squirm
(Like this pathetic bunch).

CHORUS.
310   Look sharp! Be quick! Come on!

Exeunt. Enter BLEPYROS, *dressed in women's clothes.*

BLEPYROS.
I don't understand it. Where can she have *gone*?
It's not dawn yet, and there's no sign of her.
No sign of my clothes and boots either. And me
Lying there tossing and turning, dying for a . . .
I mean, you get to feeling you're going to *burst* . . .
In the end I had to put on her dress,
320   Her shoes, and come out here to find a place to . . .
But where? Not here . . . it's a bit public .
Oh, I don't know, though. It's dark. Who's to see?

He squats.

Why did I have to take a wife, at my age?
Where's she gone? What's she up to? Ah well,
No time for that now. I've other things to do.

Enter PHEIDOLOS, *dressed in women's clothes.*

PHEIDOLOS.
Who's there? What are you doing? Heavens,
   Blepyros.

BLEPYROS (*jumping up*).
That's right . . . neighbour.

PHEIDOLOS.
What's that – a yellow dress?
330   Have you had an accident?

BLEPYROS.
What? No. It belongs to my wife.
I snatched it up . . . I had to come out
In a hurry.

PHEIDOLOS.
But where's your cloak?

BLEPYROS.
I couldn't find it, could I?

PHEIDOLOS.
Why didn't you ask your wife?

BLEPYROS.
I couldn't find her, either! She's gone . . .
Slipped out . . . disappeared. She's up to something.

PHEIDOLOS.
Well, that's amazing! It's just the same with me.
My wife's disappeared as well . . . with *my* cloak.   340
I wouldn't have minded that, but she took my shoes
As well. She must have done: these are all I could
    find.

BLEPYROS.
I know how you feel. Just look at these.
Well, I was in a hurry. I had to wear *something*.
It was these or stay in . . . and we've just put on
Clean sheets. What *can* they be up to? D'you think
They've gone to some kind of breakfast-party?

PHEIDOLOS.
Mm . . . probably. It can't be anything else.
I mean, you know my wife – she's not the type.   350
What's wrong? Are you practising a dance?
Well, never mind. It's time for the Assembly.
If only I could find my *clothes* . . .

BLEPYROS.
You go on. I'll come when I'm ready. *If* I'm ready.
I should never have eaten those hard-boiled eggs.

PHEIDOLOS.
It's a meeting to settle that big blockade.

Exit.

BLEPYROS (*muttering*).
Don't talk to *me* about big blockades.
What am I going to do? I've got to eat . . .
Where will I find the *room*? I should never
360   Have bolted those eggs . . . I'm really bolted now.
Ladies and gentlemen, is there a doctor
In the house? Or a plumber, perhaps?
Perhaps it's Amynon I need. Someone
Who knows his way around back passages.
You know Amynon. You know his motto,
'Go anywhere, do anything'. God, it's no joke.
I'm in agony. Hera, Artemis, help . . .
Send me a midwife . . . don't just leave me here.
370   What d'you think this is? The Battle of the Bulge?

He squats. Enter CHREMES, *in his own clothes.*

CHREMES.
Hello, what are you going? Having a – ?

BLEPYROS.
No, no, good heavens no.
I'm . . . well, I'm standing up.

CHREMES.
That's your wife's dress you're wearing.

BLEPYROS.
I *know* that!
It was all I could find in the dark.
What are *you* doing here, anyway?

CHREMES.
I've just come from the Assembly.

BLEPYROS.
Is it finished already?

CHREMES.
You're not joking. Right on the stroke of dawn.
You should have seen us: out before we were in.

BLEPYROS.
Did you get paid?

CHREMES.

    I wish I had. I arrived too late.   380

    The shame of it! I couldn't get in.

BLEPYROS.

    Couldn't get in? No pay? That's not like you.

CHREMES.

    There was a crowd of strangers there.

    Odd-looking, pale-faced strangers. *Very* pale . . .

    We decided they were bakers.

BLEPYROS.

    Eh?

CHREMES.

    The flour.

BLEPYROS.

    Oh.

CHREMES.

    The whole place was full of them. Rows and rows,

    Like buns on a shelf. There was no room for us.

BLEPYROS.

    No point me going, then?

CHREMES.

    You wouldn't

    Have made it at cock-crow . . . never mind now.   390

BLEPYROS.

    Ye gods! Such dreadful news! Oh me, oh my!

    I'll not get paid! I'm broke! I'm going to cry!

    You saw that play too, didn't you? Years ago.

    Aeschylus? Something about Achilles . . . ?

    Never mind. What did they want, all those bakers?

CHREMES.

    Aha, you wait and see. The day began

    With a debate on the Safety of the State.

    Well, the first speaker was Neokleides.

BLEPYROS.

    The one who squints?

CHREMES.
Exactly. He fumbled his way
To the speaker's platform, and the crowd roared,
400   'How can *he* see where we ought to go?
He can't even see the end of his own nose!'
He blinked at them a bit, and shouted back,
'All right, *you* tell me what to do!'

BLEPYROS.
That's easy.
A clove of garlic, crushed up in vinegar;
Stir in a handful of Spartan mustard,
And bung it in your eye when you go to bed.
That's what I'd have told him.

CHREMES.
The next speaker was Evaion.

BLEPYROS.
That bare-faced liar?

CHREMES.
Bare-faced, nothing. He arrived today
Stark naked. Or so we all thought. *He* swore
410   It was just that the body politic was full of holes.
'And that's the point,' he said. The crowd loved it.
'There's only one way to save the state: the rich
Must be robbed, to give to the poor. A cloak
In winter, to save the state from catching flu;
Then anyone who hasn't a blanket or a sheet
420   Gets taken to the cleaner's. That's fine for him —
And a fine for them, if they don't pay up.'

BLEPYROS.
Brilliant! We could really make a meal of it,
And make every grocer give a good square meal
To anyone who needs it — especially
That fellow down the road, who gives short change.

CHREMES.
After that, a young man jumped up . . . very pale,
Pretty . . . a bit like that pansy Nikias.

His proposal was that we hand over all
The affairs of state to women. At once   430
All those bakers started cheering and clapping . . .
Mind you, the farmers didn't like it. They groaned.

BLEPYROS.
They always do.

CHREMES.
But they didn't groan loud enough.
He shouted them down, and gave us a list
Of all the good qualities women have,
And all the bad ones *you* have.

BLEPYROS.
Me?

CHREMES.
Yes, you. He said you were a pig . . .

BLEPYROS.
Who, me?

CHREMES.
Yes, you. A selfish pig.

BLEPYROS.
Who, me?

CHREMES.
Yes, you. A selfish, mean old pig.

BLEPYROS.
Who, me?

CHREMES.
Yes, you. And all of *them* as well.

He gestures at the audience.

BLEPYROS.
We can't argue with that, at least.   440

CHREMES.
Women were stuffed (he said) with business sense
And brains, and keeping their secrets to themselves.
Men hold a meeting, and blab all over town.

BLEPYROS.
Mm. True.

CHREMES.
And women are generous (he said):
They lend each other clothes and jewels and cash
(And drinking cups); they always pay them back
Quietly, without a fuss. No lawyers,

450   No witnesses. Men *always* make a fuss.

BLEPYROS.
Mm. True.

CHREMES.
There are no women master-criminals
Or traitors or spies (he said); women are nice . . .
They're good for you, and . . . oh, lots more like
    that.

BLEPYROS.
What was his motion?

CHREMES.
That we give the state
To women to manage – he said it was
The only thing we'd never tried.

BLEPYROS.
And did we?

CHREMES.
We did.

BLEPYROS.
So women are in charge now, not men?

CHREMES.
Exactly.

BLEPYROS.
460   My wife goes out to work instead of me?

CHREMES.
And buys the food and pays the rent.

BLEPYROS.
Who groans and staggers out of bed at dawn?

CHREMES.
She does. Your groaning days are gone for good.
You roll over and fart and go back to sleep.

BLEPYROS.
But just one minute. There *is* one snag.
We're not as young as we used to be. Suppose,
Now the women are on top, they demand –

CHREMES.
What?

BLEPYROS.
Demand their oats. What if . . . we can't?

CHREMES.
Simple: they'll cut our provisions off. If food
Means oats and oats mean food, you'll have to try.   470

BLEPYROS.
But fancy being *made* to . . . It's going to be hard.

CHREMES.
A good citizen does what must be done.

BLEPYROS.
It's like what my old grandad used to say:
'You can't cross an omelette . . .'

CHREMES and BLEPYROS.
'When the stable door's bolted'.

CHREMES.
Let's hope he was right.

Noise of WOMEN, *off.*

Hey up. I'm leaving.

BLEPYROS.
Wait for me.

Exeunt. Enter WOMEN *and* CHORUS.

FIRST WOMAN.
Come on, be quick.

SECOND WOMAN.
Are we being followed?

THIRD WOMAN.

480   Any *men* around?

FIRST WOMAN.

Be careful. Walls have ears.

SECOND WOMAN.

And cobblestones have eyes.

FIRST WOMAN.

Tread firmly, like men.

THIRD WOMAN.

Don't let them find out.

SECOND WOMAN.

That would never do.

CHORUS.

Keep your cloaks pulled tight.

490   Look right. Look left. Look out.

Hurry up.

We're nearly there,

Back where it all began.

Our leader's house – Praxagora

Who made the plan and fooled the men.

Get rid of the beards. Don't hang about.

If they see us, they'll know.

Quick!

Into the shadows

500   And change. Our leader's here.

We don't want her to see

Men's clothes and beards. Get changed.

They start changing. Enter PRAXAGORA.

PRAXAGORA.

That's right. Everything's gone exactly right,

Exactly the way we planned. Quick, now:

Before any men come past and see,

Get rid of the cloaks, take off the boots,

Throw the walking sticks away.

(*to some of the* WOMEN)

You gather them up, get rid of them.   510
I want to slip into the house
Without *him* seeing me,
And put his clothes back
Just where they were before.

FIRST WOMAN.
Whatever you say. Your word is our command.

THIRD WOMAN.
You're so *clever*, darling. You know *just* what to do.

PRAXAGORA.
No, no, no. Everyone here was essential.
You know the law: one . . . *man* . . . one vote.

Enter BLEPYROS *and* CHREMES. BLEPYROS *is
still in women's clothes.*

BLEPYROS.
Ha! Praxagora. Where have *you* been?

PRAXAGORA.
What business is that of yours?

BLEPYROS.
What business of mine? Oh, very nice!   520

PRAXAGORA.
You think I've got a lover, don't you?

BLEPYROS.
What, just one?

PRAXAGORA.
Can't you tell?

BLEPYROS.
What? How?

PRAXAGORA.
Take a sniff. Go on. Where's the perfume? Well?

BLEPYROS.
Can't a woman go making love without?

PRAXAGORA.
I never do – as you should know.

BLEPYROS.
> All right, then. Where *have* you been?
> Sneaking out at dawn. And in my clothes, too.

PRAXAGORA.
> I was with a friend. All night. A woman friend.
> A pregnant woman friend. Her pains had begun.

BLEPYROS.
> Why didn't you tell me before you went?

PRAXAGORA.
> I should have asked her to hold on, I suppose?

BLEPYROS.
530   It's no way to behave. You should have said.

PRAXAGORA.
> Don't you understand, I had to *hurry*?
> The message was urgent. She couldn't wait.

BLEPYROS.
> Well, why couldn't you go in your own clothes,
> Instead of leaving me here in this nightie?
> A wreath and a candle, I'd look like a corpse.

PRAXAGORA.
> It was cold, love. You know how your poor little wife
540   Feels the cold. I needed your nice warm clothes.
> You had all those blankets. You were all right.

BLEPYROS.
> That doesn't explain the boots . . . the walking stick.

PRAXAGORA.
> I was afraid of being robbed on the road.
> I thought, if I clatter along in *his* boots . . .
> If I rattle *his* stick on the cobble-stones . . .

BLEPYROS.
> You cost me a day's pay. A whole day's pay,
> Because I couldn't get to the Assembly.

PRAXAGORA.
> Well, never mind. It went exactly right.

BLEPYROS.
What. The Assembly?

PRAXAGORA.
No darling. The baby.
But *was* there one? An Assembly, I mean.

BLEPYROS.
Of course there was. I told you yesterday.

PRAXAGORA.
Oh yes. So you did.

BLEPYROS.
And you know what's been decided?

PRAXAGORA.
No.

BLEPYROS.
Huh! It's all right for *you* now. It's all yours.

PRAXAGORA.
What, dear? The mending?

BLEPYROS.
The State!

PRAXAGORA.
What? Ours?

BLEPYROS.
The State's all yours, to govern as you please.

PRAXAGORA.
Well now, isn't that lucky?

BLEPYROS.
Eh?

PRAXAGORA.
Well, just *think*!
We can start again. No more criminals,
No more lawyers, no more courts . . .

560

BLEPYROS.
I *like* courts.

CHREMES.
Hush, man. Your wife's talking. The lady of the house.

PRAXAGORA.
No more envy, no more greed; no poverty,
No despair; no pay-up-or-else, no arguments . . .

BLEPYROS.
Fantastic! Lovely! I should live so long!

PRAXAGORA.
Oh darling, don't you believe me? All right . . .
570 I'll prove it to *you*, and I'll prove it to *him*.

CHORUS.
From a pool of intelligence deep and vast
With dedicated concentration
Give a dazzling demonstration
Of the goodies you're bringing, success built to last.

A brilliant new programme, a dazzle of light,
A master-stroke, a revelation
580 To stun us into admiration
And startle this watching audience tonight.

PRAXAGORA.
It *is* startling. Quite brilliant, and new.
If you'll drop the old ways, branch out . . .
Make experiments . . . try something new . . .

CHREMES.
Oh, don't worry. You know what we're like.
We love change. We'll try anything once.

PRAXAGORA.
Well then, listen and don't interrupt,
Or ask questions, or argue or fuss
Till I've finished. My programme is this:
ALL OUR WEALTH TO BE PUBLICLY
    OWNED.
PRIVATE PROPERTY: BANNED. NO MORE
    RICH,

NO MORE POOR. NO MORE MILLIONAIRE   590
SQUIRES, NO MORE BEGGARS. NO
    BUSINESS
TYCOONS AND NO FAILURES. EQUALITY
    RULES.

BLEPYROS (*interrupting*).
    All share equally – ? *Stand.*

PRAXAGORA (*furious*).
    Shit!

BLEPYROS.
    Not for me, thanks. *Sit*

PRAXAGORA.
    I didn't mean *that*!
    I said *listen*, and *don't interrupt.*
    Once all property's public – all land
    And all money – we'll give you a grant
    And supply you with all that you need,
    Using feminine knowhow and thrift.   600

CHREMES.
    Yes, that's fine – for the wealth you can *see*.
    But supposing a man makes his cash
    By invisible earnings, like shares . . . ?

PRAXAGORA.
    He'll declare them, like everyone else,
    Or be guilty of fraud.

BLEPYROS. *Straight*
    Just like now.

PRAXAGORA.
    But he won't *need* his money –

CHREMES.
    Why not?

PRAXAGORA.
    Because all that he wants will be *free*:
    Bread, fish, cakes, cloaks, wine, crowns, dried
      peas –

There's no reason for hoarding your cash,
610   And no reason for cheating the state.

BLEPYROS.
Did they ask for a reason *before*?

PRAXAGORA.
But those days and those laws are all gone!
In a communal state, who needs cash?

BLEPYROS.
If you fancy a pretty young girl,
Will the Common Purse give you a grant
To buy presents and take her to bed?

PRAXAGORA.
There's no need: you can sleep with her for free.
My new system, called SEX-ON-DEMAND
(GO-TO-BED-AND-MAKE-BABIES) is law.

CHREMES.
But what if we all want the *same*
Pretty girls? Does your law cover that?

PRAXAGORA.
Yes. The girls make an organised queue,
And you sleep with the ugliest first.

BLEPYROS.
But look, what about old men like me?
If it's ugliest first, I won't *last*
620   Till I've got to the end of the queue.

PRAXAGORA.
Oh, don't worry. They won't *all* insist.

BLEPYROS.
I don't get it.

PRAXAGORA.
Exactly: you don't.

CHREMES.
It's a good law for females: there won't
Be a stone left unturned. But it's no
Good for males. All the he-men get girls,
And the rest of us nothing at all.

PRAXAGORA.

    Yes you will, if you watch them and wait.
    When the tough guys and he-men go out
    To the new Common Tables, you pounce
    On their girls. It's the same law for them:
    IF YOU WANT THE WINE, THEN SQUEEZE
       THE GRAPES.

BLEPYROS.

    Ha! Lysikrates looks like a grape –   630
    He'll be squeezed?

PRAXAGORA.

    It's the law of the land.
    Democratic and equal. Just think
    Of the scene: Mr Big's with a girl,
    Showing off all his money and charm –
    And a down-at-heel weed comes along
    And takes over and says, 'Stand aside!
    When I've finished, I'll pass you the cup.'

CHREMES.

    But if that's how we're going to live,
    When a baby's born, how will it know
    Who its Daddy is?

PRAXAGORA.

    Simple: it won't.
    There'll be hundreds of Daddies: all those
    Who were adult and there at the time.

CHREMES.

    No, that's not going to work. If the young
    Treat their fathers the way they do now
    When they *know* who they are, when they *don't*
    They'll be dropping us right in the –   640

PRAXAGORA.

    No,
    It's not *like* that. You don't understand.
    In the old days, you kept out of fights
    When they didn't concern you; but now,

When we're one great big family, we'll fight
In a massive great family row.

BLEPYROS (*pointing into the audience*).
Just a minute! There's *him* . . . and there's *him* . . .
What if *they* call me Daddy? No thanks!

CHREMES.
It could be even worse.

BLEPYROS.
What d'you mean?

CHREMES.
Aristyllos the Armpit comes up
And says 'Daddy!', and gives you a kiss.

BLEPYROS.
650   That old dung-heap? He'd suffer.

CHREMES.
No, *you* would.

PRAXAGORA.
There's no chance of that. He's too old.
He won't kiss you. He knows his own Dad.

BLEPYROS.
Thank god. Have you *smelt* the man's breath?

CHREMES.
Then there's farmland. If nobody owns
Any fields, who's to dig them and plough?

PRAXAGORA.
Slaves. You've only one duty to do:
When it starts to get dark, you get dressed
And slip down to the table for dinner.

CHREMES.
But who'll make new clothes? We'll need new
    clothes.

PRAXAGORA.
When you wear out the old ones, the State
Will provide, out of public funds.

CHREMES.
   Public funds? Ah. Suppose you're in court
   And you're fined. Who'll pay that – public funds?

PRAXAGORA.
   There won't *be* any courts.

BLEPYROS (*aside to* CHREMES).
   Whoops! You're out of a job.

CHREMES (*aside to him*).
   So are you.

PRAXAGORA.
   We just don't need them now.

BLEPYROS.
   What d'you mean?
   They're essential. Non-payment of debts –

PRAXAGORA.
   There won't *be* any payment of debts.   660
   There won't *be* any debts. All our cash
   Is community property now:
   There'll be no need to borrow or lend.

CHREMES.
   Very clever.

BLEPYROS.
   But what about this?
   A community dinner ends up in a fight
   And a drunk beats you up. Well, who pays?

PRAXAGORA.
   Ah! He'll have all his rations cut off,
   And his belly will teach him good sense.

CHREMES.
   No more thieves?

PRAXAGORA.
   You can't steal what you own.

BLEPYROS.
   If you go out at night and get mugged,
   And they steal all your clothes –

CHREMES.
Sleep at home. They won't mug you in bed.

PRAXAGORA.
That's no problem: the clothes
Are *their* property too. If they ask,
670   Hand them over; next morning, go down
To the communal tailor's for more.

BLEPYROS.
No more . . . *gambling*?

PRAXAGORA.
No money: no point.

CHREMES.
It's a new kind of life.

PRAXAGORA.
Public life.
The whole city one communal house . . .
No more barriers . . . freedom for all . . .

BLEPYROS.
We will *eat* . . . ? arms & legs.

PRAXAGORA.
We'll convert all the courts
Into communal dining-rooms –

BLEPYROS.
What?
With those hard wooden benches?

PRAXAGORA.
Ideal.
When the banquets are over, a choir
Of young children will stand up and sing
All the old songs, the ones we like best –

CHREMES.
680   Very nice. And the urns . . . ?

PRAXAGORA.
We'll put those
In the market place. Then, every day,

We'll draw lots for our tables and food:
A: vegetarian,
B: honey-cakes,
C: fish
D . . .
D . . .

BLEPYROS (*sarcastically*).
D.licious. And what about M?

PRAXAGORA.
What about it?

BLEPYROS.
Em for Empty, you know.
They get nothing.

PRAXAGORA.
Of course not. There's plenty for all.   690

BLEPYROS *and* CHREMES *dream together.*

CHREMES.
Oh yes, plenty for all.
You'll get up from the table . . .

BLEPYROS.
Drunk, wearing your crown . . .

CHREMES.
You'll grab a torch, and go . . .

BLEPYROS.
And they'll be waiting for you,
Waiting in the shadows by the road.

CHREMES.
Hello, handsome. Got the time?

BLEPYROS.
Over here, lover-boy. Try me.

CHREMES.
And from an upstairs window:
*Come upstairs if you like
Honey, peaches and cream . . .*

BLEPYROS.

700 *But Mummy comes first.*
You'll have to try me first.

CHREMES.

Yes, and weedy old men
Will mock handsome young boys . . .

BLEPYROS.

Not so fast! Hold your horses!
Put her down. I saw her first.

CHREMES.

Before she drinks the wine
She has to squeeze the grapes . . .

BLEPYROS.

So get a grip of yourself, and wait!

PRAXAGORA.

You're beginning to get the idea?

BLEPYROS.

710 Oh yes.

PRAXAGORA.

Now, I have to go down to the market-place.
There's so much to do since I was elected
Chief Executive: check all incoming goods,
Hold auditions for Town Crieress,
Set up all the communal dining rooms
Ready for the feast . . .

BLEPYROS.

There's a feast already?

PRAXAGORA.

Tonight. And then there are the prostitutes:
They've got to be stopped.

BLEPYROS.

Why?

PRAXAGORA.

These ladies here:
720 We want to save all the handsome boys for them,

Not for prostitutes. No slave is allowed to shave
   herself
Or wear perfume or seductive dresses
Like her mistress. Slaves must sleep only with
   slaves.
We call it free love, because it's *for* the free.

BLEPYROS.
Go on, then. I'll walk beside you.
Then people can point me out and say,
'Look! The General's husband. What a man!'

Exeunt PRAXAGORA *and* BLEPYROS.

CHREMES.
I'm going to take all my goods and property
Down to the communal market-place. First
I want to go through them and make a list.

*He goes in. Music, dance. Then he comes out again, calling
back inside in a coaxing way, as if to a pet.*

Come on, little sieve. That's it . . . out you come.   730
Go over there, ready to lead the procession.

A SLAVE *brings out a sieve, and lays it on the ground.
Other* SLAVES *fetch the other items as* CHREMES
names them.

There we are. Aren't you holy? Just what we need
For a civic procession. Now then, who's next . . .
Who'll carry the litter? The rubbish pail,
Of course. Oh my dear, you might have washed!
Have you been with Lysikrates, that dirty old man?
I think we'll have a soap-dish next . . . that's right,
And the water-clock . . . And now, behind them . . . ?

The SLAVES *bring in a rooster, followed by a beehive.*

Hello, old cock! You going to sing for us?   740
Hello, honey! You spread yourself just there.
A vase, a three-legged stool, a vinegar-pot . . .
Ladles and jelly-spoons, bring up the rear . . .

*He starts piling the things on a handcart, ready to take out.
Enter* PHEIDOLOS, *muttering.*

PHEIDOLOS.
    Hand over my property? I'd have to be mad.
    I'll have a good look round first, and see
    How the land lies. I'm not an idiot:
750   I'm not throwing away a lifetime's toil
    Till I find out what's going on.
    Ow! What's this in aid of? Are you moving house?

CHREMES.
    No, I'm –

PHEIDOLOS.
    Going to the pawnshop?

CHREMES.
    No, I'm –

PHEIDOLOS.
    A jumble-sale?

CHREMES.
    No, I'm handing them in to the common store,
    To the market-place, as the new law says.

PHEIDOLOS.
    You're doing *what*?

CHREMES.
    That's right.

PHEIDOLOS.
760   You're crazy.

CHREMES.
    Why?

PHEIDOLOS.
    Just look.

CHREMES.
    You mean I'm crazy to obey the law?

PHEIDOLOS.
    Poor old thing – what law?

CHREMES.
    The new one, of course.

PHEIDOLOS.
That proves it. You're off your head.

CHREMES.
Off my head?

PHEIDOLOS.
You're nutty. You've flipped. You're round the
twist.

CHREMES.
To do as I'm told?

PHEIDOLOS.
And where will it get you?

CHREMES.
It's common sense.

PHEIDOLOS.
Cha! It's nonsense.

CHREMES.
Aren't you going to hand in yours?

PHEIDOLOS.
Not yet, I'm not.
I'm waiting to see what the rest of them do.   770

CHREMES.
They'll be handing them in.

PHEIDOLOS.
I believe you.

CHREMES.
But everyone says so.

PHEIDOLOS.
Says so, eh?

CHREMES.
They promised they would.

PHEIDOLOS.
Promised, eh?

CHREMES.
You don't believe *anything*.

PHEIDOLOS.
  Anything, eh?

CHREMES.
  Oh, go to hell.

PHEIDOLOS.
  To hell, eh?
  D'you really imagine they mean what they say?
  This lot? They're takers, not givers-away.
780 Even the gods want a hand-out, round here:
  If you want any favours, you grease their palms.

CHREMES.
  For heaven's sake, leave me in peace. I'm busy.
  I've got to get this lot strapped up. Where's that
     cord?

PHEIDOLOS.
  You're really going through with it?

CHREMES.
  Why else would I tie up a three-legged stool?

PHEIDOLOS.
  But it's daft!
790 Just wait, till you see what the rest of them do.

CHREMES.
  Then what?

PHEIDOLOS.
  Well then . . . wait a bit longer, of course.

CHREMES.
  For what?

PHEIDOLOS.
  An act of god . . . a fire . . . a flood . . .
  A black cat crossing the road . . . *anything*
  That might persuade you to give it up.

CHREMES.
  I'm not hanging round to come in *last.*

PHEIDOLOS.
  Don't worry: you won't be last.

CHREMES.
  I've told you. This lot here. They're *always* last.

CHREMES.
  They'll hand them in.

PHEIDOLOS.
  And if they don't?

CHREMES.
  They will.

PHEIDOLOS.
  And if they don't?   800

CHREMES.
  We'll beat them up.

PHEIDOLOS.
  And if we don't?

CHREMES.
  We'll run.

PHEIDOLOS.
  And if we don't?

CHREMES.
  Oh, go to hell.

PHEIDOLOS.
  And if I don't?

CHREMES.
  Oh, nuts!

PHEIDOLOS.
  You're quite determined? You'll really hand them
    in?

CHREMES.
  Oh yes. And look . . .

  He points into the audience.

  They're getting the idea too.

PHEIDOLOS.
  Getting the idea? Look at him. Antisthenes.

He won't move. If he sat on the pot for a month,
He wouldn't move.

CHREMES.
There are plenty of others.

PHEIDOLOS.
Like the manager, you mean? Think *he'll* move?

CHREMES.
810   Well, I've never *seen* him move . . .

PHEIDOLOS (*to the audience*).
It's no good:
He's really going through with it.

CHREMES.
Of course I am.

PHEIDOLOS.
Have you forgotten what happened *last* year?
The *last* government fiasco? All that salt?

CHREMES.
Well, yes.

PHEIDOLOS.
And devaluation – remember that?

CHREMES.
Will I ever forget it? I'd sold my grapes:
I got a good price for the whole harvest,
A bag of silver. I went into town
820   To buy a sack of corn. I put the bag down –
And they laughed in my face. 'Silver? Hard luck:
From yesterday, we're only accepting gold.'

PHEIDOLOS.
And that brilliant new tax they tried – the one
Supposed to put us in the black for good?
Remember that? A tax on bits of string.
A knotty problem: they never tied it up.

CHREMES.
But things are different, now that women rule.
830   They'll get a grip on things.

PHEIDOLOS.
They won't grip *me*.

CHREMES.
You're babbling. Slave, come here. Take the pole.

Enter TOWN CRIERESS.

TOWN CRIERESS.
People of Athens, citizens, lend me your ears.
A communiqué from the commanderess.
NOW IS THE TIME FOR ALL GOOD MEN TO
  COME
TO THE PARTY. THE TICKETS ARE FREE.
  FROM ME.
STATE OF THE LARDER: GOOD. TABLES:
  GROANING.   840
CUSHIONS AND PILLOWS: SOFT. BOWLS:
  FULL OF WINE.
WAITRESSES: READY AND WAITING. FISH:
  BATTERED.
HARE: SPITTING. CAKES: BAKED.
  CROWNS: WOVEN.
EVERYTHING'S READY, FROM SOUP TO
  NUTS.

(*in a confidential aside*)

Even Geron's ready: wrinkled boots and baggy
  cloak
Changed for party clothes and dancing pumps.
The cooks (young and pretty) are personally
  guaranteed
By Smoios: old cunning-tongue's tasted every single
  dish.   850

(*back to the main announcement*)

THE BREAD'S READY. COME AND GET
  STUFFED.
MESSAGE ENDS.

Exit.

PHEIDOLOS.
Well, excuse me.
No point standing here, when duty calls.

CHREMES.
Where are you going? You've handed nothing in.

PHEIDOLOS.
I'm going to the party.

CHREMES.
You have to hand in first.

PHEIDOLOS.
Oh, I'll hand in.

CHREMES.
When?

PHEIDOLOS.
Afterwards.

CHREMES.
What?

PHEIDOLOS.
And I still won't be the last. You wait and see.

CHREMES.
860   You're going straight to the party?

PHEIDOLOS.
I know my duty. When my country calls . . .

CHREMES.
They won't let you in.

PHEIDOLOS.
I'll go round the back.

CHREMES.
They'll still throw you out.

PHEIDOLOS.
Let them try. I'll sue.

CHREMES.
They'll laugh in your face.

PHEIDOLOS.
I'll make a stand . . .

CHREMES.
A stand?

PHEIDOLOS.
A stand. Behind the door. And pinch
The goodies as they pass me by.

CHREMES.
Just mind
You don't pinch mine. Hey, Sikon, Parmenon,
Pick up the things, and come with me.

PHEIDOLOS.
I'll help.

CHREMES.
Oh no you won't. You'll get down there, and tell   870
The Generaless they're yours. I'll manage, thanks.

Exit with his SLAVES, *taking the property.*

PHEIDOLOS.
H'm. Better think of something else. Fast.
I've got to get to the party, and still keep my stuff.
I've got it! Just a minute . . . Yes, that's it!

*He picks up an object at random from the stage – perhaps the
statue of Hermes from beside* CHREMES' *front door.*

One party-ticket. Quick . . . no time to waste.

Exit. Choral interlude. Then enter FIRST HAG.

FIRST HAG.
Where have all the young men gone? Or *any* men?
Surely I plastered enough makeup on . . .
They could hardly miss me in *this* dress.
I've a song in my heart . . . I'm ready for love . . .   880
And where *are* they? You can't grab what isn't there.
O Muses, come down here, into my mouth,
And find me some really sexy songs . . .

GIRL (*from an upstairs window*).
So you slipped out first for once, you old prune!

What are you hoping to do – squeeze *my* grapes?
Go on, I'm listening. Anything you can sing,
I can sing sweeter . . .

(*to the audience*)

What do you mean, *boring*?
This is live theatre . . . you'll find it very nice.

FIRST HAG (*mocking*).

890   *This* is live theatre . . . you'll find it very nice.
Where's the flute-player? Come on, sweetheart,
Get hold of your instrument. I'm going to sing.

Music. She sings and dances.

If you want a good time
Just get *me* into bed.
Don't sample *her* wine:
Try my vintage instead.
A young girl never understands;
She won't be true.
What you need are experienced hands:
I'll stick to you.

GIRL (*to a different tune*).

900   Fly into my nest
If you're seeking the best,
Cool caresses, soft breasts, luscious legs;
Not vinegar dregs
And a beard and bad breath –
Sex with her is like sleeping with Death.

FIRST HAG.

When you're panting with lust
May your bed-frame go bust
And your legs get the staggers and shakes;
When you pucker and kiss
May your lovers all hiss
910   And turn into a bedful of snakes.

GIRL.

Where's my lover-boy gone?

Why's he taking so long?
Am I lonely and left on the shelf?
Now that Mummy's away –

(*aside, to the wings*)

Do I *have* to go on with this?

No answer. She continues:

Now that Mummy's away
And I'm ready to play,
Must I lie back and do it myself? 920

FIRST HAG.
Oh, you're so out of luck!
You're so itchy to fuck
And you've got to play patience instead.

GIRL.
You won't chase me away,
For whatever you say
I'm much younger . . . and better in bed.

FIRST HAG (*spoken*).
Puss, puss, puss! Miaow all you like,
They won't come for you, they'll come for me.

GIRL.
With a hearse, I suppose?
Heard that one before?

FIRST HAG.
A hundred times.

GIRL.
You've heard them *all* before.
Poor . . . old . . . thing.

FIRST HAG.
Don't you worry about my age.

GIRL.
All that makeup . . . like plaster on a wall.

FIRST HAG.
What's got into you?

GIRL.

930   Nothing. What's up with *you*?

FIRST HAG.

I've got a boyfriend. Epigenes.

GIRL.

Old Father Time, you mean.

FIRST HAG.

Epigenes: you wait and see.

GIRL.

He's coming for me, not you.

FIRST HAG.

Poor little pussy!

GIRL.

Dirty old bag!

FIRST HAG.

Why not stick your head in, and wait and see?

GIRL.

I will if you will.

FIRST HAG.

I've nothing to lose.

They hide. Enter EPIGENES.

EPIGENES.

I'll curl up with a *girl*,

940   Not a bag or a hag

With one foot in the grave.

I'm a man, not a slave.

FIRST HAG (*aside to the audience*).

Well, he won't get *that* ride.

He'll be sorry he tried.

And he'll pretty soon learn

It's democracy's turn.

Even so, I'd better keep an eye on him.

EPIGENES.

I'm drunk with her, on fire for her. Oh gods,

I can't wait to get her on her own. Ohh . . . *gods*!

GIRL (*from the window, aside to the audience*).
    I've shaken her off. She's gone. Daft old bat!   950
    She really believed me. Eek! Epigenes!

    (*singing*).

    Oh, darling, come quickly,
    Let's hurry to bed.
    I'm dying to fondle
    Your nice curly head.
    I want you, I want you,
    Oh take me to bed.

EPIGENES.
    Oh darling, come quickly   960
    And open the door.
    I'm panting for kisses
    And desperate for more.
    I need you, I need you,
    Oh, take me to bed.

GIRL.
    Oh yes, my love,
    That's right, my love,
    My sweet, my love,
    My lovely love –   970

EPIGENES.
    Please stop singing and open the door.

GIRL.
    My honey-bee,
    My piece of cake,
    My magic wand,
    My crown, my jewel –

EPIGENES.
    I'm going crazy. Please open the door.

FIRST HAG (*coming forward*).
    No need to knock. I'm over here.

EPIGENES.
    Ergh! What?

FIRST HAG.
So impatient! You'll hammer it down.

EPIGENES.
Oh god . . .

FIRST HAG.
What a torch. Do you . . . want anything?

EPIGENES.
Er . . . I was . . . I was looking for a man.

FIRST HAG.
A *man?*

EPIGENES.
980   Yes. Er . . . you haven't seen him, have you?

FIRST HAG.
Now don't be silly. I *know* what you want.

EPIGENES.
Yes . . . but . . . not over a hundred . . . I can't,
I just *can't.* I was hoping . . . sort of, *twenty?*

FIRST HAG.
Poor darling! That was yesterday. Today
It's twenty last, and over-a-hundred first.

EPIGENES.
But, I mean . . . the law of supply and demand . . .

FIRST HAG.
Exactly. *I* demand . . . and *you* supply.

EPIGENES.
But *this* is the door I was knocking on.

FIRST HAG.
990   I'm sorry: you have to knock on my door first.

EPIGENES.
I want a woman, not a sack of flour.

FIRST HAG.
Oh, you're just saying that. I know you love me.
You're shy, out here in the street. Never mind:
Pucker up, there's a good boy.

EPIGENES.
But your lover . . .

FIRST HAG.
Eh? Who?

EPIGENES.
What's his name? You know . . . that sex . . .
Er . . . sex . . . that *sexton*! Dug your grave years ago.

FIRST HAG.
I know what you want.

EPIGENES.
I know what *you* want.

FIRST HAG.
The law says you're mine.

EPIGENES.
You're crazy! Put me down.   1000

FIRST HAG.
You're very hot. I'll take you up to bed.

EPIGENES (*aside to the audience*).
Don't bother with nails or hooks or glue. Use *her*!

FIRST HAG.
Flatterer. Come on, lover. Come home with me.

EPIGENES.
Oh, I forgot. I can't. Quite impossible.

FIRST HAG.
What?

EPIGENES.
The law. Ha-ha! Yes, the new law.
I can't give anything to you:
I have to give it to the State.

FIRST HAG.
That's quite all right.
I'm an official collector: you can give it to me.

EPIGENES.
But I haven't got it *with* me!   1010

FIRST HAG.
Look: see this?

EPIGENES.
Erp! What is it?

FIRST HAG.
I thought it might change your mind.

EPIGENES.
What *is* it?

FIRST HAG.
Just listen. You'll see.

She unrolls it, and reads.

BY ORDER OF THE WOMEN. SUBJECT: SEX.
SEX BETWEEN A YOUNG MALE AND A
   YOUNG FEMALE
IS PERMITTED ONLY IF EVERY ELDERLY
   FEMALE
IS SATISFIED SHE HERSELF HAS BEEN
   SATISFIED
BY SAID YOUNG MALE. PENALTY FOR
   NON-SATISFACTION:
SAID MALE'S PRIVATE PARTS TO BE
   PLACED
IN THE HANDS OF A RECEIVER (OFFICIAL,
   ELDERLY, FEMALE).
1020   BY LAW.

EPIGENES.
That's stretching things a bit.

FIRST HAG.
And that's the law.

EPIGENES.
Can't one of my neighbours stand bail for me?

FIRST HAG.
No standing, no bail. This thing's in your own
   hands.

EPIGENES.
　Suppose I'm unfit?

FIRST HAG.
　You can't withdraw.

EPIGENES.
　Supposing I *won't*?

FIRST HAG.
　You'll get a long stretch.

EPIGENES.
　What *can* I do?

FIRST HAG.
　Come home with me, to bed.

EPIGENES.
　There's no escape?

FIRST HAG.
　No hiding-place. Come on.

EPIGENES.
　All right, then. Go and get everything ready:　　1030
　The perfumed oil, the clean white sheets, the
　　flowers,
　The candles, the pot of water by the door –

FIRST HAG.
　What are you talking about? Bed or a funeral?

EPIGENES.
　It's hard to say. You may not stand the strain.

　Enter GIRL.

GIRL.
　Just a minute! Where are you taking him?

FIRST HAG.
　Home.

GIRL.
　You can't do that. You, go to bed with *him*?
　You're old enough to be his mother.　　1040
　What d'you think this is, *King Oedipus*?

FIRST HAG.
> Bitch! You're just jealous. Is that what you think
> Of the law? You'll be sorry. You wait and see.

> *Exit.*

EPIGENES.
> Oh, thank you, darling . . . thank you. Pff!
>   Saved . . .
> In the nick of time . . . a fate worse than death.
> Take me upstairs, quick. I want to . . . say
>   thanks . . .
> I want to show you my . . . gratitude.

> *Enter* SECOND HAG.

SECOND HAG.
> Hello, hello, hello. Taking liberties,
> Are we, dearie? He's to sleep with me first.
1050 > That's the law round here.

EPIGENES.
> Oh golly, she's even worse.
> Where did they dig you up, you walking corpse?

SECOND HAG.
> Walk this way.

EPIGENES (*to* GIRL).
> Don't just stand there. Do something.
> She wants me to walk that way.

SECOND HAG.
> The *law* wants you to walk this way.

EPIGENES.
> Put me down! What are you, a vampire bat?

SECOND HAG.
> Aren't you the cheeky one? Come on . . . this way.

EPIGENES.
1060 > Quick! Fetch me a potty! I've got to . . .

SECOND HAG.
> It's all right. I've a lovely one . . . upstairs.

EPIGENES.
    There isn't time for that! I'll send you up
    A couple of my friends . . .

SECOND HAG (*to* GIRL).
    Excuse me, dear.

    Enter THIRD HAG. *The* GIRL *runs inside.*

THIRD HAG.
    Ha-HA! Caught you! Just where
    Are you going with her?

EPIGENES.
    I'm not! It's rape!
    Oh please, please, whoever you are, help me.
    Kind lady, don't let me be –

    He sees her face.

    Aaaaaargh!
    Oh Herakles, Pan, Castor and Pollux,
    Don't let it get me! It's worse than them all.   1070
    What is it? The Missing Link? The Living Dead?

THIRD HAG.
    Never mind that. Come here.

SECOND HAG.
    Come *here.*

THIRD HAG.
    Don't worry. I won't let you go.

SECOND HAG.
    Neither will I.

EPIGENES.
    Leave me alone. You're pulling me in two.

SECOND HAG.
    Do as the law says, then, and come with me.

THIRD HAG.
    Not if an uglier old hag turns up.

EPIGENES.
    And what about *her*? That pretty girl in there?

> By the time you've done, there'll be nothing left
> For her.

THIRD HAG.
> That's her problem. And *this* one's mine.

EPIGENES.
1080 All right, all right. I give in. Which one first?

SECOND HAG.
> Me, of course. Come on.

EPIGENES.
> *She's* got to leave me alone.

THIRD HAG.
> It's my turn first.

EPIGENES.
> Tell that to her, not me.

SECOND HAG.
> I'm not giving up my turn.

THIRD HAG.
> Neither am I.

EPIGENES.
> Oh god!
> I'm not a fucking WISHBONE!

SECOND HAG.
> Pardon?

THIRD HAG.
> Eh?

EPIGENES.
> What good will it do, to pull me in two?

SECOND HAG.
> Oh.

THIRD HAG.
> Ah.

SECOND HAG.
> Don't fight it. You're mine.

THIRD HAG.
   I tell you he's mine.

EPIGENES.
   It's like being on the rack. STOP PULLING
      THAT!
   How can I paddle two canoes at once?   1090

SECOND HAG.
   Take some iron tablets. Quick. We're nearly there.

EPIGENES.
   Oh my god, she's winning. We're nearly there.

THIRD HAG.
   STOP!
   It's all right. I know just what to do.
   We'll *all* go in. We'll all three go to bed at once.

EPIGENES.
   Oh no, no *please*! Not all at once! I *can't*!

THIRD HAG.
   You've got to, lover. Don't make such a fuss.

EPIGENES (*to the audience*).
   Don't sit there and laugh. It's tragedy, not farce.
   I'll be treading *her* grapes half the night, and half   1100
   Making toad in the hole with *her*. Don't laugh.

   (*to the sky*)

   Zeus, what have I done? Was it something I said?
   I'm a man, not a keeper in a zoo.
   I'm in your hands . . . oh please, look after me.
   If I . . . don't make it . . . to the other side . . .
   Bury my corpse there . . . by the exit sign . . .
   And erect . . . erect a memorial stone
   In my memory . . . an angel, weeping tears
   Of grief . . .   1110

   (*in a different voice*)

   . . . or two old crows, like HER and HER!

   The HAGS *pursue him out. Short interlude. Then the*
     TOWN CRIERESS *comes in, tipsy.*

TOWN CRIERESS.
>Ladles and jellymen . . . what a nice time
>We're having . . . one and all . . . especially me.
>*Friends, neighbours, countrymen,*
>Lend me your glasses. *The quality of wine*
>*Is not strained; it droppeth . . . oh, it droppeth,*
>How it droppeth . . . in jugs and jugs and jugs . . .
>*What a lovely bouquet . . . what a pert little wine . . .*
>*I think you'll be amused by its . . .* go on,
>Pour yourself another. The night is young,
>*And these our revels now . . .* are just begun.

>Has anyone seen Himself? I'm looking for
>Himself . . . the General's husband. Mr Boss.

CHORUS.
>Stay here and wait. He won't be long.

TOWN CRIERESS.
>That's right.
>Ooh look, here he is. I think he's on his way.

>*Enter* BLEPYROS.

>Sir . . . Mr General . . . oh sir, aren't you lucky?

BLEPYROS.
>Me?

TOWN CRIERESS.
>Yes. There's no one else I'd rather be.
>There's no one luckier.

BLEPYROS.
>Why?

TOWN CRIERESS.
>It's a great big town . . .
>Hundreds and hundreds and hundreds of people.
>At least.

BLEPYROS.
>So what?

TOWN CRIERESS.
>Out of all those hundreds

And hundreds and hundreds, you're the only one
Not at the party.

CHORUS.
Lucky? That's *lucky*? How is it lucky?

TOWN CRIERESS. *cross to gasket*
Now where are you going?

BLEPYROS.
To the party, of course.

TOWN CRIERESS.
All right. But you're going to be the last, you know.
Everyone else is there. The Generaless
Told me to fetch you . . . and these young ladies . . .
There are a few bottles left, if you hurry . . .   1140

(*gesturing to the audience*)

Bring these nice people . . . they're not *all* asleep.
Let's all go . . . all go to the party.

BLEPYROS (*to the audience*). *move to Centre Stage.*
Well, did you enjoy that? A lovely speech.
She meant it, too. There's plenty to eat
For every one of you – when you get back home.
I'm going to the party. I'll just get my torch. *SL.*   1150

TOWN CRIERESS.
Don't waste time, then. Go on. Take *them* with you.
While you get ready, I'll say a few words
To whet their appetites. Is the music ready?
Exit BLEPYROS. *Music.* *DSL. DO THE TRAIN AFTER Sarah.*
A little idea for the judges.
Did you like the plot? Give *us* first prize.
Did you like the jokes? Give *us* first prize.
Have you got all that? Give *us* first prize.
I know we had to come on here first,
But that's the fault of the draw, not us.
Remember us through all the other plays: 1160
Don't act like third-rate whores, who forget
Every client they've had except the last.

(*to the* CHORUS)

Ladies, it's time. It's time, dear friends,
To pick up your feet and dance.
It's party time. Listen. Pick up the beat.

A rhythmic dance begins.

What's for dinner? There's

All come in

Mussels and oysters and crayfish
And winkles and scallops and lobster
1170   And haddock and herring and salmon
And whiting and pilchards and coley *cod*
And mullet and turtle and CRAB;

Then there's

Chicken and turkey and pheasant
And woodcock and peacock and partridge
And pigeon and plover and heron
Blackbird And song-thrush and lapwing and blackbird *thrush*
And cygnet and rabbit and DUCK;

Then there's

Cherries and peaches and apples
And raisins and cheeses and NUTS.

That's right, NUTS.

1180   What was that? You want more?
Well, then, give us the prize,
And good eating . . .

Good clapping . . .

GOODNIGHT!

Exeunt omnes.

When the dawn breaks.
Town crier Start clapping
ENTIRE Bronce with gong.
Start to Bang gong. Pull the UNTS
Sign down.

ARISTOPHANES

WEALTH

translated by Kenneth McLeish

Characters

CHREMYLOS
KARION
BLEPSIDEMOS
POVERTY
CHREMYLOS' WIFE
CITIZEN
SECRET POLICEMAN
OLD WOMAN
YOUNG MAN
HERMES
PRIEST

silent parts:

SLAVE
WITNESS

CHORUS of elderly farmers

A street in Athens. Enter WEALTH, *followed by*
CHREMYLOS *and* KARION.

KARION.
> Zeus! Ye gods! This isn't funny.
> Who'd be the slave of a lunatic?
> You give him the best advice in the world;
> He ignores it; things go wrong –
> And who gets the blame? It's your neck –
> Or that's what you thought until Sir bought you.
> The one who owns the piper calls the tune.
> The hell with it! I blame Apollo.
> Cure-all! Know-all!
> Him and his golden tripod!   10
> We go to Delphi to ask his advice,
> His Nibs and I, and what do we get?
> Sir in a foul mood, chasing a blind man
> Up the hill, down the hill, all the way home.
> It's just not natural. We're supposed to lead
> The blind, not follow them – and there's
> His lordship, chasing a white-stick merchant
> Who won't even speak, while I tag along behind.
> Well, if he's lost his tongue, I haven't.
> Why, sir? Why? I won't shut up.
> I'll be a perfect nuisance till I know
> What's going on. You can't hit me.   20
> I've still got my wreath on, from the temple.

CHREMYLOS.
> Ah, knock it off, before *I* knock it off.

KARION.
> Charming. I only asked.
> And I'll go on asking. Him, for a start –
> Who *is* he? I *am* on your side.

CHREMYLOS.
> That's right, you are.
> What's yours is mine, what's mine is yours –
> If it's not nailed down, that is.
> All right then, listen. You know me.

Honest, honourable all my life.
And where's it got me? Nowhere.

KARION.

Who's arguing?

CHREMYLOS.

30   And you know who's making it these days?
Loudmouths, temple-robbers, state informers,
    scum . . .

KARION.

Tell me about it.

CHREMYLOS.

So I went to ask Apollo for advice.
Not for me, you understand. I've had my life.
I've shot my bolt. For my little boy.
My son and heir, my one and only,
My pride and joy.
Is he on the right track,
Or should he give up honesty?
Lie, cheat, steal? That's where the money lies.

KARION.

And what did All-seeing Apollo answer?

CHREMYLOS.

40   I'll tell you his very words. 'Whomsoever
Thou clappest eyes on when thou departest hence,
Cleave unto him, don't let him get away,
Invite him home.'

KARION.

And whom did you clappest eyes on?

CHREMYLOS.

Him.

KARION.

It's obvious, then, isn't it? Apollo's advice.
For your pride and joy. 'Get with it, son.
Follow the fashion. Go with the flow.'

CHREMYLOS.

What d'you mean?

KARION.
    Ask *him*. Even a blind man can see it.
    These days, scum always rises to the top.   50

CHREMYLOS.
    There must be more. No oracle's that simple.
    We'll ask him who he is and why he's here
    And what he wants. What's in it for us?
    We'll unravel the oracle. We'll find the clue.

KARION (*to* WEALTH).
    What's your name? Want a fist up the throat?
    Speak up.

WEALTH.
    Get knotted.

KARION.
    Funny name.

CHREMYLOS.
    No finesse, have you? No savoir faire.   60
    Watch this.

    (*to* WEALTH)

    Sir, as one man of the world to another,
    I wonder if you'd introduce yourself.

WEALTH.
    Get stuffed.

KARION.
    Apollo's message. Loud and clear.

CHREMYLOS (*to* WEALTH).
    There's nothing to worry about.
    Tell us your name –

KARION.
    - or get a teeth sandwich.

CHREMYLOS.
    Well?

WEALTH.
    Jump over a cliff, the pair of you.

CHREMYLOS.
 Pfui.

KARION.
 It's not a bad idea, sir. Let's stack
 Him on a cliff, and stand and watch
70 While he falls and breaks his neck.

CHREMYLOS.
 Grab hold.

WEALTH.
 No! Please!

CHREMYLOS.
 So what's your name?

WEALTH.
 If I tell you, you'll be even worse.
 You'll never let me go.

CHREMYLOS.
 Of course we'll let you go. Any time you like.

WEALTH.
 How about now, then? Put me down.

CHREMYLOS.
 Oh. There.

WEALTH.
 Listen. I was hoping to keep this dark.
 But since you ask so persuasively . . .
 My name is – Wealth.

CHREMYLOS.
 You bastard! Wealth, and you keep it dark?

KARION.
80 Wealth? Dressed like that? Ye gods!
 Apollo, Ares, Athene, Hera, Hermes, Zeus,
 You, Wealth?

WEALTH.
 Yes.

CHREMYLOS.
 Himself?

WEALTH.
Himselfest.

CHREMYLOS.
But why are you so pasty-faced?
Where've you been?

WEALTH.
Inland Revenue. Rebate Office. Locked away.

CHREMYLOS.
Doing time! But why?

WEALTH.
Zeus did it. Out of spite for mortals.
When I was young and keen, I told him
I'd only go round with honest, decent people.
Nice people. So he blinded me,   90
To stop me knowing them when I saw them.
Zeus has it in for nice.

CHREMYLOS.
But it's nice people who worship him.
They're the only ones.

WEALTH.
You explain it.

CHREMYLOS.
Suppose you got your sight back?
Would you still go round with crooks and sharks?

WEALTH.
Silly question.

CHREMYLOS.
You'd plump for honest?

WEALTH.
I've pined for honest, all these years.

CHEMYLUS.
Ha! So have I – and I can see.

WEALTH.
Let me go now. I've told you who I am.   100

CHREMYLOS.
Oh no. You're ours, and ours you stay.

WEALTH.
I knew it. I said you were trouble.

CHREMYLOS.
Trust me. Please stay.
I'm the honestest person you'll meet round here.
The only one, in fact.

WEALTH.
They all say that till I give them gold.
Then you see what swine they really are.

CHREMYLOS.
110   Not everyone. Surely.

WEALTH.
Every bloody one.

KARION.
Cheeky bastard!

CHREMYLOS.
Look: stay with us, you're made.
Bright sunshine every day. Bright sunshine . . .
Got it! Are you listening? Stay with us,
For a start, you get to see again.

WEALTH.
No thanks. Why should I want to see again?

CHREMYLOS.
What?

KARION.
The stupid bastard *likes* being blind.

WEALTH.
I don't. But if Zeus got to hear,
120   He'd make me squirm.

CHREMYLOS.
Worse than now, you mean? You *like*
Stubbing your tootsies on cobblestones,
Walking into walls?

WEALTH.
  I'm scared of him.

CHREMYLOS.
  You still don't get it.
  God of gods, chicken of chickens!
  If you get your sight back, even for five minutes,
  Zeus and his thunderbolts can stuff themselves.

WEALTH.
  Shh! He might be listening.

CHREMYLOS.
  What if he is?
  You're far more powerful than he is,
  And I can prove it.

WEALTH.
  How?

CHREMYLOS.
  No problem.
  Karion, why is Zeus king of the gods?   130

KARION.
  Because he's the wealthiest.

CHREMYLOS.
  And who provides his wealth?

KARION.
  This twit here.

CHREMYLOS.
  When people sacrifice, what do they ask for?

KARION.
  Wealth. No messing.

CHREMYLOS.
  You made Zeus what he is,
  And you could finish him tomorrow.

WEALTH.
  How?

CHREMYLOS.
  Just tell 'em: no more sacrifices.

No barley cakes, no oxen, nothing.
Unless you say so.

WEALTH.
Why would they listen?

CHREMYLOS.
Barley cakes, oxen . . . they don't grow on trees.
People buy them. So if you cut off the cash . . .

140   Let Zeus put one foot wrong, he's done for,
And it's you that does for him.

WEALTH.
You're saying, it's thanks to *me*
They sacrifice to Zeus?

CHREMYLOS.
Exactly. And you're essential in other ways.
Necessities. Life's little luxuries.
Wealth makes the world go round.

KARION.
Take me for instance.
Free man . . . debt . . . no money . . . slave!

CHREMYLOS.
Take tarts. Corinthians. Ladies of the night.

150   Poor man . . . forget it. Rich man . . . open wide.
Or so they tell me.

KARION.
Take boys. Bottoms up, darling?
First pay the service charge.

CHREMYLOS.
The kind of boys *you* know. Not gents.
Not little gents.

KARION.
They ask for something else?

CHREMYLOS.
Yes. Horses. Hunting dogs.

KARION.
Call it rough or smooth, I call it trade.

CHREMYLOS.
Who sponsors arts and crafts? You do.   160
It's for you that A makes shoes . . .

KARION.
B bangs metal, C knocks wood . . .

CHREMYLOS.
D works gold (the gold he gets from you) . . .

KARION.
E works houses, F works public baths . . .

CHREMYLOS.
G's a fuller . . .

KARION.
H shampoos blankets . . .

CHREMYLOS.
I's a tanner . . .

KARION.
J sells onions . . .

CHREMYLOS.
K sleeps with L,
And has to pay M (the husband) N (the fine) . . .

KARION.
All down to you.

WEALTH.
I am important, aren't I? I'd no idea.

KARION.
There's more. All these depend on you –

CHREMYLOS.
The Great King of Persia, His Mincing Majesty.   170

KARION.
All those Great Queens who run our Parliament . . .

CHREMYLOS.
The Athenian navy . . .

KARION.
Those sailors from Corinth . . .

CHREMYLOS.
Pamphilos . . .

KARION.
His little friend . . .

CHREMYLOS.
Each master of arts . . .

KARION.
Each master of farts . . .

CHREMYLOS.
Thanks to you, Egypt got the Pyramids laid down.

KARION.
Thanks to you, Philonidas got Lais laid down.

CHREMYLOS.
You paid for Timotheus' tower . . .

KARION.
180   That mighty erection . . .

KARION.
Who wins wars? The ones with Wealth.

CHREMYLOS.
All down to you. Everything that happens,
Good, bad, all down to you.

WEALTH.
I never realised. I do all that?

CHREMYLOS.
There's more. No one ever has enough of you.
People get fed up with other things.
Love, for example . . .

KARION.
190   Cheesecake . . .

CHREMYLOS.
Poetry . . .

KARION.
Porridge . . .

CHREMYLOS.
  Honour . . .

KARION.
  Treacle pudding . . .

CHREMYLOS.
  Courage in battle . . .

KARION.
  Figs . . .

CHREMYLOS.
  Ambition . . .

KARION.
  Custard . . .

CHREMYLOS.
  Command . . .

KARION.
  Bean soup . . .

CHREMYLOS.
  But no one's ever fed up with you.
  Give people 30 drachs, they ask for 60.
  Give them 60, they must have 103,
  Or their lives are ruined.

WEALTH.
  You're very convincing. There's just one thing.

CHREMYLOS.
  What?

WEALTH.
  All this power. I'm not sure I can handle it.   200

CHREMYLOS.
  Chicken of chickens! I told you so.

WEALTH.
  What d'you mean, chicken?
  Just because I keep myself to myself.
  Locked in a cupboard. They break in,
  Find nothing, say I'm scared.
  I call it insurance, forward planning.

CHREMYLOS.
Never mind all that. Are you with us?
We'll get your sight back.
210   Eagle-vision: easy.

WEALTH.
How? You're mortals.

CHREMYLOS.
Aha! Apollo said . . .   You remember Apollo?
Prophet. Laurel-shaker.

WEALTH.
Apollo's in on this?

CHREMYLOS.
Couldn't be inner.

WEALTH.
No!

CHREMYLOS.
There you go again.
I've told you, I'll fix everything.
Even if it kills me.

KARION.
Me too. Help, that is.

CHREMYLOS.
And there are hundreds more of us.
Little people, with justice in their eyes
And nothing in their pockets.

WEALTH.
220   Fat lot of use they'll be.

CHREMYLOS.
Nonsense. You can put that right before we start.
Karion, don't just stand there.

KARION.
Sorry. What?

CHREMYLOS.
Fetch my fellow-farmers.

Poor hard-working souls.
They'll be toiling in the fields.
Tell them to hurry, if they want
Their share of Wealth.

KARION.
I'm off. Take this inside, will you?
Part of the sacrifice. A bit of leg.

CHREMYLOS.
All right. Get on with it.

Exit KARION.

Now, Wealth, my dear old god,   230
Why don't you step inside? My little house.
All you have to do is fill it with money.
Fair means, foul, no questions asked.

WEALTH.
Oh gods!
I hate going into strange people's houses.
It's trouble, every time.
Misers stuff me in the cellar,
And when their friends ask for a loan,
Just a little glimpse of me
Till the end of the week,   240
'Wealth?' they shout, 'Wealth?
Never heard of him!'   High-spenders
Are even worse. They make me pass my time
With whores and dice, and I'm stripped,
Stark naked, chucked in the street,
Before you can blink your eye.

CHREMYLOS.
It's obvious then, isn't it? You need
Someone ordinary, middle-of-the-road.
Like me. Fond of saving – who isn't?
Fond of spending too, when I get the chance.
Come on. I want my wife to meet you,
And my son, my one and only, my pride and joy,
The apple of my eye (apart from you).   250

WEALTH.
    Very funny.

CHREMYLOS.
    Would I lie to you?

    He takes him inside. Music. Enter KARION *and*
        CHORUS.

KARION.
    For goodness' sake hurry, dear workmates
        and friends of my master.
    Hard-working and honest –
        why can't you run faster?
    Your future's before you: health,
        happiness, all that you need.
    Put a spurt on. Don't dawdle.
        Quick! Show me some speed.

CHORUS.
    My dear fellow, we're coming,
        and coming as fast as we're able.
    We're older than you, and our limbs
        aren't too stable.
    But why are we running?
        What's happening? Why all the fuss?
    What does Chremylos want?
260   Why the hurry? Why us?

KARION.
    I keep telling you. Why don't you
        listen? Your troubles are over.
    No grumbles, no worries,
        You're living in clover.

CHORUS.
    How on earth can that be?
        How does Chremylos know, for a start?

KARION.
    There's a guest in the farmhouse.
        A smelly old fart.
    Hairless, toothless, bent, shrivelled

and thick.
Not even a foreskin. A clapped-out,
  pathetic old prick.

CHORUS.
But you told us of treasure. You boasted
  of bliss.
Heaps of happiness. Holidays.
  Nothing like this.

KARION.
What a pain old men are! I've had them
  up to here.
As much as I can take. No more!
  No fear!　　　　　　　　　　　　　　270

CHORUS.
So what did you call us for?
  Damn silly trick!
You'll be sorry. You'll pay for it.
  Hand me my stick.

KARION.
You don't get it yet, do you?
  You don't use your brain.
So I'm playing silly beggars?
  D'you think I'm insane?

CHORUS.
Don't give yourself airs. Every whip,
  Every chain
In the house calls out 'Karion!',
  Promising pain.

KARION.
Well, if that's how you feel,
  you can go straight to hell.
Now nothing on Earth
  will persuade me to tell.

CHORUS.
Cheeky bastard! D'you think we've got
  nothing to do

But come cross-country running
   just to please *you*?
280
'Emergency!' That's what you said.
   Spit it out!
What's the matter? What's happening?
   What's it about?

KARION.
  Oh, all right then, I'll tell you.
    I ought to be fair.
  The old bastard is Wealth –
    and he's willing to share.

CHORUS.
  Share with *us*? You mean Wealth –
    after all these long years – ?

KARION.
  You can all be King Midas.
    Just grow asses' ears.

CHORUS.
  I believe you at last. What a glorious day!
  What luck! What a wonderful chance!
  I've got to sing. I've got to dance.

290 KARION.
  I'll dance a Cyclops dance and lead the way.

    He and the CHORUS *sing and dance.*

  O follow me, tarantara,
  O follow, follow me.
  O billygoats and sheep that play
  In meadows all the livelong day,
  Your master the Cyclops is calling,
  Tarantara, tarantara,
  Your master the Cyclops is calling.

CHORUS.
  We'll follow you, tarantara,
  We'll follow, follow you.

And when you're dozing, drunk with wine,
We'll carry out our grand design:
We'll sharpen a treetrunk and blind you,
Tarantara, tarantara,   300
We'll sharpen a treetrunk and blind you.

KARION.
O follow me, tarantara,
O follow, follow me.
Then I'll be Circe, charm you all
To grunting porkers in a stall,
Going 'Wee-wee-wee' home to your mummies,
Tarantara, tarantara,
Going 'Wee-wee-wee' home to your mummies.

CHORUS.
We'll follow you, tarantara,
We'll follow, follow you.
And when you're Circe, weaving spells,
We'll tie you up, for all your yells.   310
You'll go 'Wee-wee-wee' home to your mummy,
Tarantara, tarantara,
You'll go 'Wee-wee-wee' home to your mummy.

KARION.
We're here now. Stop your song.
The journey wasn't long.
Dance to the door and knock.
Give Chremylos a shock.
I'm going round the back
For a snack.
I need all my strength today
To act this play,
Tarantara, tarantara,   320
To act this flipping play.

Exit. The CHORUS *dance. When they finish,*
   CHREMYLOS *comes out.*

CHREMYLOS.
My dear fellows, you came!

How kind. How quick.
No time to say hello.
We've done all that.
Let's get busy and save the god.

CHORUS.
No problem.
I'll give 'em my Gorgon glance.
Remember the Assembly, how we push
330   And shove in the expenses queue?
Just wait till we get our hands on Wealth.

CHREMYLOS.
Here's Blepsidemos. At the double.
He must have heard as well.
Just look at him run!

Enter BLEPSIDEMOS.

BLEPSIDEMOS.
What's going on? Where, and how,
Has Chremylos found all this cash?
Everyone knows: the barbers' shops
Are full of it. 'Your mate's
Made a fortune overnight.'
340   If it's true, why tell the neighbours?
Very unAthenian.

CHREMYLOS.
I'll share it with him as well.
Blepsidemos, wonderful news.
I've made a fortune, since yesterday,
And I'm going to share it all with you.
My dear old friend . . .

BLEPSIDEMOS.
It's true, then? You really are wealthy?

CHREMYLOS.
I will be soon, if the god agrees.
There's no profit without risk.

BLEPSIDEMOS.
What risk?

CHREMYLOS.
  What d'you mean, what risk?

BLEPSIDEMOS.
  What *risk*?

CHREMYLOS.
  The usual. If it works, we're made.   350
  If it doesn't – phut!

BLEPSIDEMOS.
  I don't like this at all.
  Nobody makes a fortune overnight.
  Have you done something you shouldn't?

CHREMYLOS.
  What d'you mean?

BLEPSIDEMOS.
  Robbed a temple? Nicked the offerings?
  And now you're sorry?

CHREMYLOS.
  Good god, of course not.

BLEPSIDEMOS.
  Come off it. I can tell by your face.   360

CHREMYLOS.
  Cross my heart.

BLEPSIDEMOS.
  I knew it! It's always the same.
  Love of loot destroys us all.

CHREMYLOS.
  You're off your head.

BLEPSIDEMOS.
  Oh no. Not me, mate. You.

CHREMYLOS.
  You've gone all gloomy and thoughtful.

BLEPSIDEMOS.
  Look me in the eye. Go on.
  You can't. That proves it.

CHREMYLOS.
>Got it! All this cawing and croaking.
>You want a cut.

BLEPSIDEMOS.
370   A cut? What of?

CHREMYLOS.
>I keep telling you, you've got it wrong.

BLEPSIDEMOS.
>You mean it wasn't a temple?
>You mugged someone.

CHREMYLOS.
>Bloody hell!

BLEPSIDEMOS.
>Conned them?

CHREMYLOS.
>Trust me.

BLEPSIDEMOS.
>What did you do?
>For heaven's sake own up.

CHREMYLOS.
>You're taking me to court,
>And there isn't a crime.

BLEPSIDEMOS.
>Court, is it?
>Give me three hundred drachs.
>I'll slip them to the clerk.
>No case, no hassle, no gossip.

CHREMYLOS.
380   Lawyer-talk! Three hundred spent,
>Twelve hundred on the bill.

BLEPSIDEMOS.
>I can see it all.
>A poor, pathetic figure in the dock,
>With an olive-branch in one hand
>And his wife and children in the other.

Rather like Pamphilos' picture of *The Suppliant
Ladies*.

CHREMYLOS.
You still don't get it.
I'm going to enrich honest, decent citizens.
Deserving cases. The little people.

BLEPSIDEMOS.
You've nicked as much as that?

CHREMYLOS.
Why can't you get it straight?

BLEPSIDEMOS.
Look who's talking. Straight!   390

CHREMYLOS.
I've got Wealth inside, you fool.

BLEPSIDEMOS.
It's where it came from that worries me.

CHREMYLOS.
The god of Wealth.

BLEPSIDEMOS.
Eh?

CHREMYLOS.
Inside.

BLEPSIDEMOS.
In the house?

CHREMYLOS.
Precisely.

BLEPSIDEMOS.
You?

CHREMYLOS.
Me.

BLEPSIDEMOS.
Wealth?

CHREMYLOS.
Wealth.

BLEPSIDEMOS.
Rubbish.

CHREMYLOS.
Gospel.

BLEPSIDEMOS.
Cross your heart?

CHREMYLOS.
And spit in your eye.

BLEPSIDEMOS.
Swear by the gods?

CHREMYLOS.
Name 'em.

BLEPSIDEMOS.
But if you've got Wealth, inside,
Why don't you spread him round?

CHREMYLOS.
What d'you mean?

BLEPSIDEMOS.
Share him out.

CHREMYLOS.
Ah! Later.

BLEPSIDEMOS.
400   What?

CHREMYLOS.
There are things to do first.

BLEPSIDEMOS.
Such as?

CHREMYLOS.
Getting his sight back.

BLEPSIDEMOS.
Whose sight?

CHREMYLOS.
Whose d'you think?

BLEPSIDEMOS.
You mean . . . he's really blind?

CHREMYLOS.
As a piece of cheese.

BLEPSIDEMOS.
That's why he never noticed me!

CHREMYLOS.
He will now, if the gods agree.

BLEPSIDEMOS.
What do we do? Call a doctor?

CHREMYLOS.
In Athens? Can you afford the fee?

BLEPSIDEMOS (*to the audience*).
Ladies and gentlemen, is there an optician . . . ?

CHREMYLOS.
That lot? Don't waste your time.

BLEPSIDEMOS.
You're right.

CHREMYLOS.
I've got it all worked out.   410
We'll take him to the Hall of Healing.
The Temple of Asklepios.
If they can't help him there, who can?

BLEPSIDEMOS.
What will he have to do?

CHREMYLOS.
Just lie there overnight.

BLEPSIDEMOS.
Is that all? What are we waiting for?

CHREMYLOS.
Karion!
Enter KARION.

KARION.
You called?

CHREMYLOS.
Fetch the god,
And a mattress and some blankets.
Bring them to the Temple of Asklepios.
We're going there now.

KARION.
The Hall of Healing? Right.

Exit.

BLEPSIDEMOS.
Come on, then.

CHREMYLOS.
I'm coming.

BLEPSIDEMOS.
Faster!

CHREMYLOS.
This is as fast as I can manage.

Enter POVERTY.

POVERTY.
STOP!
Ye criminals! What foul intent
Have ye afoot? I come, heav'n-sent,
To stop it. Stand! Be silent. Hear me,
Or else I'll give ye cause to fear me.

BLEPSIDEMOS.
Herakles!

POVERTY.
You bastards! What a thing to do!
I've really got it in for you.
420   How could you dare? How could you risk it?
This really, really takes the biscuit.

CHREMYLOS.
'Who art thou, wench, alone and palely loitering?'

BLEPSIDEMOS.
Shh! Look at her face. It's the Demon Queen
From some Greek tragedy.

CHREMYLOS.
No footnotes.

BLEPSIDEMOS.
She won't get far.

POVERTY.
Just a minute! Who do you think I am?

CHREMYLOS.
Brothel-keeper?

BLEPSIDEMOS.
Foghorn?

CHREMYLOS.
She's loud enough.

BLEPSIDEMOS.
I'm cowering.

CHREMYLOS.
What have we done to you?

POVERTY.
You're trying to chuck me out. Bastards!
It's not very nice. You're dumping me.   430

CHREMYLOS.
Can't you dump yourself? The nearest cliff?
Who are you, anyway?

POVERTY.
A poor, wronged soul am I.
You did it. Sob and sigh.

BLEPSIDEMOS.
She's that barmaid from up the road –
The one who gives short measure.

POVERTY.
Nay, Poverty am I, your friend
In days when ye had naught to spend.

BLEPSIDEMOS.
Apollo! Gods above! Excuse me . . .

CHREMYLOS.
Where are you going? Coward. Wait.

BLEPSIDEMOS.
No fear.

CHREMYLOS.
440   What's wrong with you?
There's one of her, and two of us.

BLEPSIDEMOS.
Didn't you hear? She's Poverty. The worst.
The pits. The living dead.

CHREMYLOS.
Stand still.

BLEPSIDEMOS.
No fear.

CHREMYLOS.
Wealth needs us. He's relying on us.
Who else has he got? He's all alone.
We can't leave him stranded just because of her.
We've got to stay and fight.

BLEPSIDEMOS.
Fight? Fight? What with?
450   Have *you* a shield or a breastplate?
Didn't *she* make you pawn them, years ago?

CHREMYLOS.
Don't panic. Wealth can handle that.
Wealth can handle her. No problem.

POVERTY.
I've caught you in the act,
You swine – and that's a fact.

CHREMYLOS.
Oh, shut up. We haven't touched you.

POVERTY.
Doing me a great big favour, are you,
Giving Wealth his sight back?

CHREMYLOS.
    No. Not you. The whole human race.   460

POVERTY.
    The human race, a favour? What, exactly?

CHREMYLOS.
    Kicking you out. What d'you think?

POVERTY.
    Kicking me out? You're joking.
    There's nothing worse you could do for them.

CHREMYLOS.
    There is. We could let you stay.

POVERTY.
    I do far more good than Wealth. I'm essential
    To human happiness, and I can prove it.   470
    If I can't, do what you like to me.

CHREMYLOS.
    You're wasting your time.

POVERTY.
    No, you are. Giving honest people money?
    What're you thinking of? You're off your trolley –
    And I can prove that too.

BLEPSIDEMOS.
    A-aa-aah!

POVERTY.
    Yelling already! We haven't even started.

BLEPSIDEMOS.
    What else d'you want me to do, when I hear
    Such rubbish? How else do I shut you up?

POVERTY.
    Try listening.

CHREMYLOS.
    Suppose you don't convince us?   480
    What then?

POVERTY.
    Whatever you like.

CHREMYLOS.
Fair enough.

POVERTY.
So long as it's the same for you, if you lose.

CHREMYLOS.
Death, twenty times over?

BLEPSIDEMOS.
Once is enough for me.

POVERTY.
Get on with it! Prove me wrong?
I can hardly wait.

CHORUS.
It's contest time! Fight! Fight!
Quick, furrow your brow,
Don't flinch, be bright.
Fight! Now!

CHREMYLOS.
It's simple. Cash! Reserve it
490   For honest people who deserve it.
And as for crooks, who carve
Their way with crime: let the bastards starve!
How do we do it? All we need
Is a single dazzling, daring deed.
Give Wealth his sight. He'll lose
That low-life scum. You'll see!
He'll choose
God-fearing folk, like you and me.

BLEPSIDEMOS.
One nil! You win!

CHREMYLOS.
500   The way we live now: don't pretend it's
Not crazy. Don't try to defend it.
Every citizen honest and true
Is forced to cohabit with you –
Not the peak of ambition.

And there's no way to change the position,
Unless we help Wealth,
And he helps us himself,
Gives us money to make the transition.

POVERTY.
You daft old fool! If Wealth could see
You'd lose the benefits you get from me.
If everyone was wealthy, who   510
Would work? Would you? Would *you*?
No arts, no skills. No one to build
Your ships, or write your poetry, or gild
Your statues, tan your leather, mend your shoes.
Your farms would die. Who'd dig and weed
If they could choose
To do nothing instead? There'd be no need.

CHREMYLOS.
We've slaves. They'll do just as they're told.

POVERTY.
They won't if they're loaded with gold.

CHREMYLOS.
We'll get others. We'll buy 'em.

POVERTY.
And who will supply 'em?

CHREMYLOS.
Pirates, working for profit.   520

POVERTY.
Come off it!
They'll be counting their treasure,
Not serving your pleasure.
Plough, plant, hoe – don't you see
That if once you dump me
And choose Wealth
You'll be crippling yourself?
Oh, you'll suffer, far worse than before.
No bed-makers: sleep on the floor.
No carpets then,

No perfumes. When
530   Your daughter's wedding comes, no dress.
You'll be rich, and in total distress
With none of the luxuries of life.
Fear of *me* fills each working man's head
When he looks at his kids and his wife.
Yes, it's me makes him work, sets him
   earning his bread.

CHREMYLOS.
So those are the blessings you bring!
No wonder we whistle and sing.
Haggard wives, starving children,
   fleas, bedbugs and lice;
Draughty houses, infested with
540   underfed mice;
Straw mattresses, stinking and old;
Cracked windows that let in the cold;
Our food shrivelled radishes, cabbage and bones;
Our chairs broken barrels, our pillows hard stones –
It's not much fun
For anyone
Whose life is a series of pitiful moans.

POVERTY.
No hopers? Don't give me the blame.

CHREMYLOS.
No hopers, paupers – just the same.

POVERTY.
550   You can't compare them. Chalk and cheese!
No hopers starve. My people seize
Their chances. Keen and fit,
They make the best of it:
Work hard, save hard. No waste, no fat.
Lean living – where's the harm in that?

CHREMYLOS.
Fantastic! Scrape and scrimp and save –
Then die, and you can't afford a grave.

POVERTY.
> You can laugh how you like: I don't mind.
> But I'm serious. Wealth's better blind.
> His cronies are greasy, pot-bellied
> > and crippled with gout.
> Mine are wiry, iron-muscled, and know
> > what hard living's about.   560
> They're awake day and night, they know
> > just what to do –

BLEPSIDEMOS.
> The buggers are muggers – and all thanks to you.

POVERTY.
> Politicians. When first they take office
> They're skint, they rule fairly and well.
> Then they find where the government trough is,
> Start guzzling, and make our lives hell.   570

CHREMYLOS.
> Overstated, but true –
> Unexpected from you.
> But it's still not enough.
> On your bike! We've got Wealth now.
> Who'll miss you?

POVERTY.
> Don't bluster and huff.
> Stop talking so tough
> And get down to discussing the issue.

CHREMYLOS.
> Right! Tell me why nobody backs you.

POVERTY.
> Because I'm so good for them! Daddies
> Know best, but when *your* Daddy smacks you
> To stop you from naughtiness,
> > my how you cry!

CHREMYLOS.
> And does Zeus know what good is and bad is?

He's rolling in wealth up there,
   high in the sky.

BLEPSIDEMOS.

580   While sending us *you*. What a pain!

POVERTY.

Are you blind? Are you lame in the brain?
Oh, for heaven's sake, let me explain.
Zeus is poor. One example. First prize
At the ancient Olympics: not gold,
Not silver. Olive-leaves, clammy and cold.

CHREMYLOS.

So the prize is mingy!
All that proves is, Zeus is stingy.

POVERTY.

590   What, miserly? Zeus? He's got Wealth
And won't share it? Do watch what you say.
He might hear you – so bad for your health.

BLEPSIDEMOS.

Oh, put on these olive-leaves. Get on your way.

POVERTY.

You admit it, then? Poverty's best?

CHREMYLOS.

Just one last simple test.
Ask the gods. At their altars. Who buys
Every sacrifice? Wealth does. Who tries
To run off with the offering? You do.
You're a jinx, you're a hex, you're a hoodoo.
I'll tell
You some news:
In this fight, when you win, you still lose.

600   So stop moaning. Get stuffed. Go to hell.

POVERTY.

O town of Argos, hear,
Oh shed a tear.

CHREMYLOS.

There's no more to say.

Get on your way.

POVERTY.
Alack! O woe!

CHREMYLOS.
For god's sake go.

POVERTY.
Where to? Do tell.

CHREMYLOS.
To hell.

POVERTY.
You'll want me back one day.

CHREMYLOS.
Just go away.   610
Just give me the pleasure
Of counting my treasure.
You silly cow,
Go now!

Exit POVERTY.

BLEPSIDEMOS.
She's gone! Now for that life of ease.
Relax, do as you please.
Happy children, smiling wife –
The only life!
Out to the baths each day,
Then home to dinner. On the way
Poor people, Poverty their boss.
Fart in their faces! Who gives a toss?

CHREMYLOS.
Come on. To the Hall of Healing.   620
To see how Wealth's been getting on.

BLEPSIDEMOS.
Quick as you like,
Before someone else turns up to stop us.

Exeunt. Choral dance. Then enter KARION.

KARION.
Ladies and gentlemen! Athenians!
Your bread and water days are done.
630   It's happiness time. Rejoice!

CHORUS.
I think he's brought good news.
Most welcome of slaves, what is it?

KARION.
His lordship's plan has worked!
Wealth can see. Asklepios did it!
The lights are on again.

CHORUS.
Good news! Oh shout and sing —

KARION.
That's right, force yourselves.

CHORUS.
Glad praises to our saviour king.
Asklepios, lord of light,
640   Whose healing hand, so fair and bright —

Enter CHREMYLOS' WIFE.

WIFE.
What's all the noise about?
Good news at last?   I've been waiting inside for
    ages.

KARION.
Quick, madam, quick. Bring wine.
I've brought you a wonderful present.

WIFE.
Where?

KARION.
I'm telling you.

WIFE.
I'm listening.

KARION.
Pin back your ears. Behold,

I shall a tale unfold –   650

WIFE.
Don't you unfold your tail to me.

KARION.
Not my tail. My *tale*.

WIFE.
Get on with it.

KARION.
We got to the temple, Wealth and I.
What a specimen! Filthy, crabby,
Nothing like the two-year-old he is now.
First off, I took him to the beach
And washed him.

WIFE.
Poor bastard! Cold seawater all over.
What a start.

KARION.
Then up we went, to the Hall of Healing.
Cakes and incense on the table.   660
'Hail to thee, Holy Fire' – all that.
I tucked Wealth in bed, the way they tell you.
We all unrolled our blankets –

WIFE.
All of you? There were other people there?

KARION.
Hundreds, and every one diseased.
Hopeless cases. Neokleides – see what I mean?
The attendant put the lights out,
And told us to go to sleep.
Whatever we heard, we weren't to say a word.   670
So there we lay, in rows like herrings.
I couldn't get to sleep. There was an old woman,
Three rows down, with a pot of soup.
I couldn't get it out of my mind.
I was holding myself in –
You know how it is when you need the pot.

Then suddenly I saw a priest
At the holy table, gathering up
The cakes and figs people had left there.

680   He went round the altars in a circle,
Consecrating the offerings into his knapsack.
'Aha', I thought. 'So that's how it's done!'
I made a beeline for the soup.

WIFE.
Fool! What if the god had noticed?

KARION.
I was dead afraid he *would* notice,
And get there first.
'Give way to anyone in a garland' –
That's what the priest had told us.
The old woman heard me and tried

690   To grab me. I hissed like a sacred snake,
Snapped at her hand. She jerked it back
Under her blanket, and lay there
Farting like a polecat.
I snaffled the soup and went back to bed.

WIFE.
And did Asklepios turn up?

KARION.
Later on, yes. And when he did,
I farted right in his face.
How could I help it? All that soup!

WIFE.
700   That's when the trouble started?

KARION.
Well, his slaves weren't pleased.
Placebo blushed; Panacea held her nose.
After all, it's not ambrosia I fart.

WIFE.
And his worship?

KARION.
Didn't even notice.

WIFE.
  Dirty beggar.

KARION.
  Used to it. Always poking around in shit.

WIFE.
  What?

KARION.
  Looking for germs.
  Anyway, I wasn't taking any chances.
  I wrapped myself in my cloak and lay still.
  He went on his rounds,
  Examining the patients in order.
  The slaves went after him, carrying   710
  A pestle and mortar and a medicine box.

WIFE.
  Stone? Like in the statues?

KARION.
  How do I know? A *medicine* box!

WIFE.
  How could you see? Inside that cloak?

KARION.
  Through the moth-holes. What d'you think?
  The first one he dealt with was Neokleides.
  Mixed up a poultice – garlic, fig-juice, vinegar –
  And plastered it on his eye,   720
  Rubbing it well in, underneath the lid.
  Neokleides jumps up, roaring and howling,
  And Asklepios says, 'I thought you liked
  Being plastered!'

WIFE.
  A joke with every cure.

KARION.
  Next he sat down by Wealth. He held his head,
  And wiped his eyes with a linen cloth.
  Panacea covered Wealth's head,   730

And all his face, with a purple towel.
Asklepios clicked his tongue
Like this – *kik, kik*! –
And two gigantic serpents slid from behind the
    altar.

WIFE.
Snakes alive!

KARION.
Exactly. They slithered under the towel,
And licked Wealth's eyes – so far as I could see.
And before you could swallow
A couple of pints, madam, quick as you are,
Wealth jumped up, and he could see again.
I started clapping and shouting –
740   And at once the god and the snakes
Disappeared behind the altar.
You can imagine what it was like
When all the sick people clapped eyes on Wealth.
Singing, shouting, dancing.
I said two big thankyous to the god:
For making Wealth see again
And making Neokleides blinder than before.

WIFE.
Asklepios, be thanked!
And where's Wealth now?

KARION.
On his way.
750   He could hardly get through the crowd.
All the honest people, the little people
Who never had two drachs to rub together,
Crowding round, trying to shake his hand.
And the ones who were rich before,
Screwing up their faces and making the evil eye.
Look, here they come: dancing,
Wearing garlands, laughing like children.

(*to the revellers offstage*)

That's right, enjoy yourselves!   760
Make the most of it. Leap and skip and sing.
You'll never go short again!

WIFE.

Oh Karion! I want to garland you,
Reward you for bringing such happy news.

KARION.

Be quick, then. They're nearly here.

WIFE.

I'll sprinkle Wealth with roses,
To welcome those brand-new eyes.

KARION.

I can't wait to shake his hand.   770

Enter WEALTH, CHREMYLOS *and* CHORUS.

WEALTH.

Good morning to the sun, and next,
My golden Athens, land of Kekrops,
City of Athene queen of heaven.
I blush for my former life. I'd no idea
What sort of people I was going round with.
I never saw the ones who deserved my friendship.
Blind and foolish, I admit it.
But now I proclaim to everyone:
I've changed my ways.   780
I never enjoyed being friends with criminals,
And I never will again.

CHREMYLOS.

Leave me alone! Fair-weather friends.
Get out of it! Stop patting me.
Don't kiss my feet. Who did that?
Has anyone not said 'Good morning'?
Anyone not tried to shake my hand?

WIFE.

Darling husband! Darling, darling Wealth!
Let me shower you with roses . . .

WEALTH.

790 Not here. Not now. I hate being showered.
In any case, *I* should be showering *you* –
With blessings. Just wait till I get inside.

WIFE.
No roses?

WEALTH.
Inside, perhaps. Not here.
This isn't a farce. Think of the critics.
Think of our learned author. You'll be throwing
Nuts and figs to the audience next.

WIFE.

800 I get you: no vulgarity. Look: Dexinikos
Is halfway out of his seat already.
Must be all those figs.

Exeunt. Choral dance. Then enter KARION.

KARION.
It's marvellous!
Don't you think it's marvellous?
We haven't spent a thing, and we're rolling.
Haven't hurt a fly, and we're in clover.
There's something about being rich –
Flour-bins brimming,
Oil-barrels oozing,
Wine-tubs swimming,
Brimming and boozing –

810 There's something about being rich.
Every mug and jar in the house,
Every salt-pot and vinegar-jug,
Has turned from china to gleaming bronze –
Except that stained old fish-service
(You know the one): that's silver now.
Ivory lamps.
We play shove-halfpenny with solid gold.
No more stones these days to wipe our bums:
It's garlic leaves or nothing.

Master's going round the house
With a garland on,   820
Collecting a sacrifice:
Ox, porker, goat, fat ram.
I had to come out. The smoke!
My eyes just won't stop watering.

Enter CITIZEN *and* SLAVE.

CITIZEN.
Come on. Don't dawdle.
We'll never find the god.

KARION.
Who wants him?

CITIZEN.
Someone who's climbed from rags to riches.

KARION.
An honest man!

CITIZEN.
Exactly.

KARION.
So what d'you want?

CITIZEN.
I want to say thank you.
Tell the god my story.
My father left me a little money.
I used it to help my friends.
Any time. No questions asked.   830
Seemed like a decent way to live.

KARION.
Don't tell me: the cash ran out.

CITIZEN.
You said it.

KARION.
You ended up skint.

CITIZEN.
You said it.

I thought they'd be happy to pay me back.
Help me like I helped them. No chance.
They looked away, said I wasn't even there.

KARION.
Big joke.

CITIZEN.
You said it.
All I had left was holes.

KARION.
But not any more.

CITIZEN.
840   That's why I want to find the god.
Say thanks.

KARION.
What's that your servant's carrying?
Cloak or fishing net?

CITIZEN.
My old cloak: my offering to Wealth.

KARION.
Fancy material. Bought for some festival?

CITIZEN.
Thirteen years ago. I've shivered in it ever since.

KARION.
These shoes?

CITIZEN.
They've been around.

KARION.
They're for Wealth as well?

CITIZEN.
Exactly.

KARION.
He *will* be pleased.

Enter SECRET POLICEMAN *and* WITNESS.

POLICEMAN.
  Gone! Every penny! Up in smoke!   850
  I'm ruined.
  Ruined, ruined,
  Ruined, ruined, ruined.

KARION.
  What *is* he trying to say?
  What on earth's the matter?

POLICEMAN.
  That bloody god! He's stripped me naked,
  Pulled my house down round my ears.
  Give me five minutes in court, five seconds!
  I'll see him blind again.

CITIZEN.
  You get the feeling something stinks.   860
  One of those rotten apples your master talks about.

KARION.
  He certainly looks like something off a tree.

POLICEMAN.
  Where is he? Where's the god who swore
  He'd make us wealthy if he got his sight back?
  Wealthy? That's a joke.

KARION.
  What's the problem?

POLICEMAN.
  Do I look wealthy to you?

KARION.
  What are you? Mugger, thief?

POLICEMAN.
  If anyone's a thief, it's him!   870
  He's stolen all I own.

KARION.
  Got it! Security police. Poor soul.
  Are you hungry? Is that why you're raving?

POLICEMAN.
> You're under arrest.
> You'll be broken on the wheel till you confess.

KARION.
> Get stuffed.

CITIZEN.
> I get down on my knees to Wealth,
> For ridding Greece of sods like you.

POLICEMAN.
880   Who asked you? His accomplice, are you?
> Where did you get that cloak?
> It's not the one you were wearing yesterday.

CITIZEN.
> I've bought some garlic. You don't scare me.

POLICEMAN (*to* WITNESS).
> Insulting behaviour. Write that down.
> Illegal Assembly. They're up to something.

KARION.
> Something bad for you.

POLICEMAN.
> You're going to have dinner, aren't you,
890   On the money you stole from me?

KARION.
> Do me a favour. The pair of you.
> Go over there, blow yourselves up, and burst.

POLICEMAN (*to* WITNESS).
> The accused denied everything.
> I can smell the evidence, inside.
> Hnf hnf!
> Grilled fish, roast goat . . .
> Hnf hnf . . .
> Lamb shish kebab.
> Hnf hnf..

KARION.
> What a dreadful cold!

CITIZEN.
Well of course! Wearing rags like those.

POLICEMAN.
It's your fault, Zeus!
Don't you see them mocking me?
A decent man, a patriot. 900

CITIZEN.
A patriot? You?

POLICEMAN.
Who else?

CITIZEN.
Prove it.

POLICEMAN.
What?

CITIZEN.
Are you a farmer?

POLICEMAN.
You're joking.

CITIZEN.
D'you make things?

POLICEMAN.
Good god, no.

CITIZEN.
You're a shopkeeper?

POLICEMAN.
Sometimes. In the line of duty.

CITIZEN.
What duty?

POLICEMAN.
Undercover. State affairs, my friend.
And personal affairs . . .

CITIZEN.
But why?

POLICEMAN.
Vocation, I suppose.

CITIZEN.
You *are* a burglar!
910   Rummaging in other people's lives.

POLICEMAN.
Someone has to do it. It's obvious, dummy.
For the sake of the state . . .

CITIZEN.
You meddle for the state?

POLICEMAN.
I see that people keep the laws.
If they don't, I punish them.

CITIZEN.
But don't we have law-courts? Juries?

POLICEMAN.
They still need evidence.

CITIZEN.
They get it.

POLICEMAN.
Of course they do. From me.
The system depends on me.

CITIZEN.
920   No wonder it's collapsing.
Look, why not retire?
Dunsnitchin. Out to grass.

POLICEMAN.
Grass? Grass? D'you take me for a sheep?
I can't give it up. It's in the blood.

CITIZEN.
No deal?

POLICEMAN.
Not for all the Wealth in Athens.

CITIZEN.
OK then. Strip.

KARION.
He means you.

CITIZEN.
Get 'em off.

KARION.
He still means you.

POLICEMAN.
Who'll make me?

KARION.
Me, for one.

POLICEMAN.
Unprovoked assault! Help! Rape!   930

KARION.
Well, you should know.

POLICEMAN.
Where's my witness? Write this down.

KARION.
He legged it hours ago.

POLICEMAN.
I'm done for. Help!

KARION.
Stop yelling.

POLICEMAN.
I'm freezing.

KARION (to CITIZEN).
Where's that old cloak? Just what he needs.

CITIZEN.
It's for the god. It's holy.

KARION.
Holey, exactly. You can't dress Wealth
In rubbish like this. But him? It's perfect.   940

CITIZEN.
What about the shoes?

KARION.
> Give them here. I'll use them
> To bash his face in.

POLICEMAN.
> Oh no you don't. I'm going.
> But I'll be back. And so will my friends.
> We'll settle this god of yours.
> Democracy must survive.
> The enemies of the state must perish.
> Nothing must be done
> Without written permission from the council.
950 Keep off the grass . . .

> *Exit.*

CITIZEN (*calling after him*).
> Now you've got my cloak and shoes,
> Have my place as well. In the bathhouse.
> Sponger in chief, beside the fire.

KARION.
> They know rotten apples when they see them.
> They'll grab his balls and heave him out.
> That's that, then. Time to go inside.
> You've words to say to Wealth.

> *Exeunt. Choral dance. Then enter* OLD WOMAN.

OLD WOMAN.
> Excuse me. Is this the right house?
960 The one where the new god is?
> Or have I taken a wrong turning somewhere?

CHORUS LEADER.
> This is the place, sweetheart. You've arrived.

OLD WOMAN.
> I'll knock and fetch someone out.

> *Enter* CHREMYLOS.

CHREMYLOS.
> It's all right. I'm here.
> What is it? What's the matter?

OLD WOMAN.
Everything's the matter.
As soon as your god got his sight back,
I lost the only reason I had for living.

CHREMYLOS.
You're a lady spy?   970

OLD WOMAN.
Good god, no.

CHREMYLOS.
A muggeress?

OLD WOMAN.
Don't be so cheeky.
What's happened is no joke.

CHREMYLOS.
What *has* happened? Get on with it.

OLD WOMAN.
It's my lover. Such a charming boy.
No cash, but pretty. And so good-hearted!
Did everything I asked. Gave total satisfaction.
Me too. It was tit for tat.
He only had to ask.

CHREMYLOS.
What did he ask for?   980

OLD WOMAN.
Peanuts. Twenty drachs for a cloak,
Eight for a pair of shoes,
New dresses for his sisters,
A cloak for his mother,
A cartload of corn.

CHREMYLOS.
You said it. Peanuts.

OLD WOMAN.
You don't understand. He loved me for myself.   990
Every time he wore the cloak, he said,
He'd think of me.

CHREMYLOS.
  I believe you.

OLD WOMAN.
  But now the rascal's changed.
  Not the same sweet boy at all.
  I sent him royal jelly and oysters,
  To build up his strength,
  With a note saying 'Come tonight'.

CHREMYLOS.
  And – ?

OLD WOMAN.
  He sent back a carrot,
1000 And a note saying 'Work it out yourself'.

CHREMYLOS.
  It's always the same.
  When a man's dying of hunger, he gnaws
  On any old crust. But when he's gold to spend . . . !

OLD WOMAN.
  What d'you mean, old crust?
  He was round at my place day and night,
  Panting for it.

CHREMYLOS.
  For what? Your funeral?

OLD WOMAN.
  Just to hear my voice.

CHREMYLOS.
  And his pocket-money chinking.

OLD WOMAN.
1010 Whenever I felt sad,
  He called me his duck, his turtle-dove.

CHREMYLOS.
  Then he asked for the shoes.

OLD WOMAN.
  He was so jealous!
  If anyone so much as glanced at me

In the carnival procession,
He beat me black and blue.

CHREMYLOS.
I bet that warned them off.

OLD WOMAN.
He said I'd lovely hands.

CHREMYLOS.
Especially full of cash.

OLD WOMAN.
I smelled so sweet.   1020

CHREMYLOS.
That *is* champagne you drink?

OLD WOMAN.
My eyes were like limpid pools.

CHREMYLOS.
Good swimmer, eh?
He could certainly do the crawl.

OLD WOMAN.
You can see why I feel betrayed.
Your god promised to help good people.

CHREMYLOS.
He'll do anything. Name it.

OLD WOMAN.
I want my darling boy nice to me again.
Or to pay me what he owes.
It's only fair.   1030

CHREMYLOS.
I thought he was paying instalments,
One each night.

OLD WOMAN.
He said he'd never leave me as long as I lived.

CHREMYLOS.
You *are* still alive? You've checked?

OLD WOMAN.
  I'm worn away with suffering.

CHREMYLOS.
  Gone to seed, more like.

OLD WOMAN.
  I'm skin and bones.

CHREMYLOS.
  Who's arguing?

OLD WOMAN.
  Look! Over there. It's him!
  Torch, olive-crown . . .
  He must be going to a party.

CHREMYLOS.
1040 I think he's been, already.

  Enter YOUNG MAN, *tipsy.*

YOUNG MAN.
  Hey, give's a kiss.

OLD WOMAN.
  What did you say?

YOUNG MAN.
  Oh, it's you, pussy-cat.
  My, aren't you grey?

OLD WOMAN.
  That's right, insult me.

CHREMYLOS.
  Be fair. He hasn't seen you for years.

OLD WOMAN.
  What d'you mean? He saw me yesterday.

CHREMYLOS.
  In that case he's different from everyone else:
  He sees more clearly when he's had a few.

OLD WOMAN.
  It isn't that at all. He always was a cheeky devil.

YOUNG MAN.
Poseidon, pussy-cat, you've gone all wrinkly.   1050
Your face is like a prune.

OLD WOMAN.
Ow! Mind that torch!

CHREMYLOS.
Yes, be careful. One spark in the wrong place,
She'll go up like last year's thatch.

YOUNG MAN.
Let's play a game.

OLD WOMAN.
What? Here?

YOUNG MAN.
Yes. Hold these nuts.

OLD WOMAN.
I beg your pardon?

YOUNG MAN.
Guess-how-many.

     (to CHREMYLOS)

You start. How many teeth?

CHREMYLOS.
That's easy. Four? Three?

YOUNG MAN.
One, and that's a stump.

OLD WOMAN.
You don't love me any more, putting me down   1060
In front of all these people.

YOUNG MAN.
Putting you down? Now there's a thought.

CHREMYLOS.
Give her a chance. Take another look.
Under all that makeup . . . such lovely bones.

OLD WOMAN.
Bastard! At your age, too.

YOUNG MAN.
  What's the matter?
  Is he feeling you up behind my back?

OLD WOMAN.
  No, he isn't.

CHREMYLOS.
1070 No, he bloody isn't. Show more respect.
  Such a lovely creature.

YOUNG MAN.
  I love her like a mother.

CHREMYLOS.
  That's just the problem. What about that message?

YOUNG MAN.
  What message?

CHREMYLOS.
  The carrot. 'Work it out yourself.'

YOUNG MAN.
  I tell you what. Don't let's quarrel.

CHREMYLOS.
  Pardon?

YOUNG MAN.
  You're older than I am. I respect you.
  I wouldn't do this for just anyone.
  But . . . she's yours.

CHREMYLOS.
1080 Steady. You can't give her up like that.

OLD WOMAN.
  Just let him try.

YOUNG MAN.
  Who asked you?

  (to CHREMYLOS)

  She's so . . . second-hand.
  Talk about the Thousand and One Nights.

CHREMYLOS.
  If you pour the tea, you have to drink it.

YOUNG MAN.
  Dregs and all?

CHREMYLOS.
  You should have used a strainer.

YOUNG MAN.
  I'm going inside.
  I want to offer Wealth these crowns.

OLD WOMAN.
  Yes, I want a word with Wealth as well.   1090

YOUNG MAN.
  Ah! I don't think I'll bother . . .

CHREMYLOS.
  What's wrong? D'you want to withdraw?

YOUNG MAN.
  I've been trying to withdraw for years.

OLD WOMAN.
  Oh get inside! I'm right behind.

CHREMYLOS.
  You can say that again!
  What do you look like? Give him air!

  Exeunt. Choral dance. Then enter HERMES. *Before he
  can knock on the door,* KARION *storms out.*

KARION.
  Who's that hammering? I heard you.
  No one? That door, knocking itself again.
  I'll teach it.

HERMES.
  Karion. Cooee.

KARION.
  You, was it?   1100
  Banging like a maniac. What d'you want?

HERMES.
> I would have banged, but you came first.
> Look, dash inside and fetch your master,
> His wife, his kids, his slaves, his dog, his pig,
> And you.

KARION.
> What? Why?

HERMES.
> Just do it. Zeus has his mincer out.
> You'll all be hamburger. Grilled in hell.

KARION.
> He wouldn't.

1110 Are you sure you've got that right?

HERMES.
> Of course I've got it right. And of course he would,
> After what *you've* done to *him*.
> As soon as Wealth could see, all offerings
> Dried up. Everywhere. No incense, no laurel,
> No barley-cakes, no sacrifices. Nothing.

KARION.
> What d'you expect?
> After the way *you* treated *us*!

HERMES.
> It's not the others I mind about. It's me.
> I'm *wasting*.

KARION.
> What a shame.

HERMES.
1120 I used to do so nicely, in every bar and caff.
> Figs, wine-cakes, honey-biscuits. Nice, not naff.
> Titbits for Hermes. Goodies for god. Not any more.
> Now it's 'He's here again. Quick, slam the door!'

KARION.
> And when we looked after you,
> What did you do for us?
> It's supposed to be two-way trade.

HERMES.
  Oh god, the scones!

KARION.
  All gone.

HERMES.
  Ah me, the ham!

KARION.
  No comment.

HERMES.
  The liver! The kidneys!   1130

KARION.
  It's a guided tour.

HERMES.
  A siplet of wine!

KARION (*fetching a potty*).
  Here. Filtered specially.

HERMES.
  I *am* on your side.
  Can't you scrounge me something?

KARION.
  What, for example?

HERMES.
  A bread-bun, round and yeasty.
  A sliver of sacrifice.

KARION.
  No chance.

HERMES.
  For old times' sake.
  When you nicked those tarts
  From Chremylos, who kept watch?   1140

KARION.
  You got your rake-off. Tart for tart.

HERMES.
  You ate them all before I got there.

KARION.
What about when he caught me?
I don't remember blow for blow.

HERMES.
It was you liked discipline, not me.
Do be friends. Do take me in.

KARION.
What d'you mean? Leave heaven,
1150   And move in here?

HERMES.
It's so much nicer.

KARION.
Desert your comrades?

HERMES.
Go where the food is, that's my motto.

KARION.
But what do we need that you could do?

HERMES.
I could be the doorkeeper. Lovely uniform.

KARION.
I know. It's mine.

HERMES.
A statue, then? If I stand like this . . .

KARION.
Not even a hatstand.

HERMES.
A lamp? I glow in the dark.

KARION.
1160   I guessed.

HERMES.
I've got it: culture.
Wealth's bound to be sponsoring
Exhibitions, festivals. He'll need
A minister of the arts.

KARION.

    I knew you'd get it. In you go.

HERMES.

    You mean it?

KARION.

    Certainly do. You can start in the privy.
    Some fine examples of local art.
    Bring me a cultural report, in triplicate –
    After you've scrubbed them off.   1170

    Exeunt. Choral dance. Then enter PRIEST.

PRIEST.

    Excuse me. Is this where Chremylos lives?

    Enter CHREMYLOS.

CHREMYLOS.

    How are you, father?

PRIEST.

    Starving to death, now Wealth can see.
    Me, the priest of Zeus our Heavenly Father.

CHREMYLOS.

    What's the problem?

PRIEST.

    No one's sacrificing.

CHREMYLOS.

    Why not?

PRIEST.

    No need. They've got everything they want.
    In the old days, when people were poor,
    There was always someone: a sea-captain
    Safely home, a defendant acquitted in court,   1180
    A private celebration – I made house calls.
    Now, nothing! No invitations,
    No offerings – except from those bastards
    Who creep into the crypt to crap.

CHREMYLOS.

    You could instal a turnstile . . .

PRIEST.
>I want to give up Zeus our Heavenly Father,
>And move in here.

CHREMYLOS.
>Ha! 'God moves in a mysterious way'.
>Zeus our Heavenly Father arrived this afternoon.

PRIEST.
1190
>You're joking!

CHREMYLOS.
>We're going to the Acropolis.
>A big procession.
>Put Wealth in the Treasury, where he lived before.
>They're coming. Take this torch and lead the way.

PRIEST.
>Just watch me!

CHREMYLOS.
>We're ready. Bring the god!

Music. Everyone comes out of the house in procession, leading
WEALTH.

OLD WOMAN.
>Hey! What about me?

CHREMYLOS.
>You carry the pots. On your head.
>Like a Caryatid.

OLD WOMAN.
1200
>Not that. The . . . favour . . . I came for.

CHREMYLOS.
>He'll be round as usual, after dark.

OLD WOMAN.
>In that case, hand me the pots.

She joins the procession.

CHREMYLOS (*to the audience*).
>Is it my fault she looks like an ice-cream cone?

CHORUS.
It's time to go.
To close the show.
Dance after me.
Right? One, two three . . .

Exeunt omnes.

MENANDER

THE MALCONTENT

translated by J Michael Walton

Characters

The god PAN
CHAEREAS, a parasite
SOSTRATOS, a young man in love
PYRRHIAS, his slave
KNEMON, a malcontent
HIS DAUGHTER
GORGIAS, Knemon's step-son
DAOS, Gorgias' slave
SIKON, a cook
GETAS, a slave in Sostratos' family
MOTHER OF SOSTRATOS
SIMICHE, Knemon's slave
KALLIPPIDES, Sostratos' father
PLANGON (non-speaking), Sostratos' sister
MYRRHINE (non-speaking), Knemon's former
  wife
ATTENDANTS
CHORUS

There are a number of minor breaks in the manuscript.
Where linking text has been inserted, this appears in
brackets.

ACT 1

Phyle, a village outside Athens. The houses of KNEMON
and GORGIAS *with, between them, a shrine to the god*
PAN. *Enter* PAN.

PAN.
   We are in Attica. Suppose it so for now.
   The village of Phyle, and for all Phylesians,
   This shrine from which I entered is sacred to the
      Nymphs.
   The locals farm this stony waste somehow, and
      it's a holy place.
   Here to my right, your left, lives Knemon,
   A malcontent, if ever there was one,
   Hostile to allcomers, cranky in all company.
   'In all company' did I say? Never in his life
   Has this Knemon volunteered a friendly word
   To anyone, never made overtures to a living soul.   10
   Bar me, and with Pan as a neighbour, he has little
      option.
   He can hardly ignore a god and pass him by,
   Though that upsets him for the day, I have no
      doubt.

   Nevertheless,
   A man like this got married once, to a widow,
   Recently bereaved and with a baby to support.
   He fought with her, day in, day out,
   And most of the night as well, like cat and dog.
   Somehow they had a daughter; which only made
      things worse.   20
   The relationship went sour to the point of no
      return.
   And she didn't. She left him, went to live with her
      son,

The one from the previous marriage, who, as it
    happens,
Lives here on the other side, eking out a living
On the smallest of smallholdings,
For his mother, himself and a single faithful slave.
He's a good lad, wise beyond his years.
'Nothing matures like experience', as they say.
The old man has the daughter but otherwise lives
    alone

30   Except for a woman slave, older than he is.
All his days are working days, digging, carting
    wood
And hating everyone in sight, his wife, his
    neighbours
In a ten mile radius, down to the very last, the lot.

The girl, though, is an innocent,
So protected there's not a mean thought in her
    head.
And paying homage to the Nymphs of the shrine,
She respects Pan too, that's me.
So she's our special care.
There's a young man, son of a local farmer

40   Who's well-to-do, owns a lot of property.
The boy's fond of the city-life but he's come here
    to hunt
With a companion. As luck would have it,
He's right here, right now, and, by a touch of
    magic,
Has fallen in love.

There's the plot. Watch, if you will,
How it develops. Please do.
Ah, here they come, I believe, and what do you
    think
They're talking about? Precisely so:
Love, about falling in love.

Exit PAN. *Enter* SOSTRATOS *and* CHAEREAS,
    a parasite.

CHAEREAS.

Tell me again, Sostratos. You saw a girl, a free girl, 50
going into the shrine with some garlands for the
nymphs and by the time she came out, you were in
love.

SOSTRATOS.

By the time she came out, yes.

CHAEREAS.

As quick as that. Or did you decide to fall in love?

SOSTRATOS.

Don't mock. I'm in a terrible state.

CHAEREAS.

I don't doubt it.

SOSTRATOS.

I brought you in on it because I thought you would
be sympathetic and because you're a bit of a fixer.

CHAEREAS.

Quite right too. That's me to a T, Sostratos. Say a
friend has fallen for some tart or other. Call for me
and I'll abduct her. No problem. Get drunk. Burn
down a door. Refuse to listen to reason. Act first, ask 60
questions later. Your frustration's a terrible thing.
'Soonest gratified, soonest pacified'. If it's marriage
you're talking about and a free girl, well that's
another matter. You wouldn't recognise me. I check
up on her family connections, financial status,
habits. I hand over a complete portfolio, a proper
record of how reliable I am.

SOSTRATOS.

Mmm. Yes, impressive. But not quite what I had in
mind.

CHAEREAS.

Let's hear the problem, then. 70

SOSTRATOS.

First thing this morning I sent my man Pyrrhias –

you know Pyrrias, the one I take hunting – I sent
him off.

CHAEREAS.

Off? Off where?

SOSTRATOS.

Off to see the girl's father, or whoever's head of the
household.

CHAEREAS.

Oh dear, oh dear.

SOSTRATOS.

Yes, it wasn't very clever, I see that. It's not really a
job for a slave. 'Love and judgement are poor
bedfellows'. I can't for the life of me think where he's
got to. I told him to discover the lie of the land and
80   come straight home.

Enter PYRRHIAS.

PYRRHIAS.

Gangway. Mind your backs. I'm coming through.
There's a loony after me.

SOSTRATOS.

What the hell . . . ? Pyrrhias . . .

PYRRHIAS.

Scatter.

SOSTRATOS.

What is it?

PYRRHIAS.

Clods of earth. Slinging them at me. Stones. I'm all
in.

SOSTRATOS.

Slinging them at you? Now where are you off to, you
little devil?

PYRRHIAS.

What? Whew. Maybe he's called off the chase.

SOSTRATOS.

Nobody's after you, for God's sake.

PYRRHIAS.

I could have sworn he was.

SOSTRATOS.

What are you talking about?

PYRRHIAS.

We've got to get out of here. Please.

SOSTRATOS.

And go where?

PYRRHIAS.

As far as possible from that front door. That man
you sent me to see. He's a psychopath, out of his
tree. What a business. I've broken half my toes.   90

SOSTRATOS.

Damnation. Is the fellow drunk or what?

CHAEREAS.

Plainly.

PYRRHIAS.

Would that I were. I'm all in. Keep on the lookout.
Oh, I can hardly speak. Run out of puff. What I did
was, I knocked at this door here and said that I
wanted to speak to the master of the house. Out
came some superannuated old biddy who came over
here, where I'm standing now, and pointed him out   100
to me up there on the ridge, wandering about
looking for wild pears to pick till he could pick a wild
quarrel with me.

CHAEREAS.

I don't like the sound of that. What then, old fellow?

PYRRHIAS.

I headed off across the field towards him. Not
wanting to intrude and intending to show him my
intentions were friendly, I stopped a little way off
and called out to him 'Oy, Dad, I've come on
business and I'm in a hurry'. And quick as a flash,
he replied 'Do you realise you're on private

110   property, you poxy devil? What do you want?' And
        he picked up a clod of earth and slung it at me, full in
        the face.

CHAEREAS.

The devil he did.

PYRRHIAS.

Then while I had my eyes closed and was swearing
back at him a bit, he picked up a piece of fencing and
belted me with it. 'What's your business with me,
then?', he kept asking and 'What's wrong with the
public road?', shouting away at the top of his voice.

CHAEREAS.

He sounds like a lunatic, this farmer.

PYRRHIAS.

Finally, I ran off and he ran after me, chasing me
round the ridge for about two miles, then down into
120   the wood flinging stones and lumps of earth at me.
And when he ran out of them, he started throwing
his pears. What a savage. Crazy old fool. Please, I
beg you. Let's go.

SOSTRATOS.

Like cowards?

PYRRHIAS.

I don't think you realise. We're in trouble here. He'll
eat us alive.

CHAEREAS.

I do really think he may have just been a little bit
upset just now. As a result of which, I do really
think, Sostratos, it would be a good idea to put off
seeing him for the time being. Discretion and valour,
you know, that sort of thing.

PYRRHIAS.

You're right there.

CHAEREAS.

He often is hypersensitive, you find, your poor
130   farmer, not just this one. They're all the same.

Tomorrow, at dawn, I'll come back and have a quiet word with him. In his own home. And you'd better head off to your home. This'll sort itself out.

PYRRHIAS.

Fine.

Exit CHAEREAS.

SOSTRATOS.

He was just looking for an excuse and glad to find it. It was abundantly clear he had no wish to accompany me, and doesn't want me to get married, if it comes to that. And as for you, I hope you rot in hell.　140

PYRRHIAS.

What did I do?

SOSTRATOS.

You damaged his land. Pinched something probably.

PYRRHIAS.

Pinched something?

SOSTRATOS.

I'm meant to believe he just upped and hit you for doing nothing?

PYRRHIAS.

Yes he did. And here he comes. I'm off, thanks very much. You talk to him.

Exit PYRRHIAS.

SOSTRATOS.

Would that I could. I'm completely useless the moment I open my mouth. What do you say to a man like this? Lord, he doesn't look exactly sociable. Somewhat formidable. Maybe I'll move away from his front door a little. That's better. Gracious. He's all by himself but he's shouting. That's not a　150 particularly healthy sign. God, I'm terrified. Why not admit it?

Enter KNEMON.

KNEMON.

Perseus was the lucky one and no mistake. Twice over. He had wings. He could fly. He never had to meet people, walking about. And if he did meet people he had this device for turning them into stone. How about that, eh? I could do with one of them. The world would be full of statues. Every-
160   where. God, what a life. People! They talk to you. They wander all over your land. I haven't got time to stand around gossiping, for Heaven's sake. I've given up trying to farm this bit altogether. They've driven me out. Passers-by. I'm a refugee. Now they chase me up the hill. In droves. Oh, for God's sake. Look at that, will you? Here's another of them. At the front door. Just standing there.

SOSTRATOS.

You don't suppose he'll hit me, do you?

KNEMON.

Is there no privacy? You couldn't find a quiet spot
170   to commit suicide.

SOSTRATOS.

Is it me he's annoyed with? I arranged to meet someone here, old chap. Just waiting for him.

KNEMON.

What did I tell you? What do you think this is, a pedestrian precinct? The War Memorial? Use my front door, why don't you, if you want to arrange an assignation? Why don't I change everything about out here? Dedicate a bench. No, wait. I'll have a shelter built. You can use it as your headquarters. It hurts, you know that? Persecution, that's what I call it.

Exit KNEMON *into his house.*

SOSTRATOS.

Complicated, that's what I call it. This requires the
180   subtle approach, I think. It certainly does. Maybe

I'd better fetch Getas, my father's slave. Yes, by
God, I will. He's hot stuff at all this intriguing and
what have you. He's had enough experience. He'll
soon exorcise this demon, no problem. I'll not let the
grass grow under my feet. A lot can happen in a day.
Whoops, there's his door again. Someone's coming
out.

Enter KNEMON's daughter carrying a pitcher.

DAUGHTER.
It would happen to me. What am I going to do?
Nurse was fetching water and she's dropped the   190
bucket down the well.

SOSTRATOS.
Good lord. Heavens above. I can't fight it. She's
gorgeous.

DAUGHTER.
He just told me to go and put the kettle on.

SOSTRATOS.
I'm quite overcome. Well, wouldn't you be?

DAUGHTER.
If he finds out, he'll kill her. Not a moment to lose.
Nymphs, dear Nymphs, I'll have to get my water
from you. As long as there isn't a sacrifice going on.
I'd hate to interrupt.

SOSTRATOS.
Allow me. I'd be delighted to fill your pitcher for
you. Won't be a moment.   200

DAUGHTER.
Would you? Oh, thank you so much.

SOSTRATOS.
There's something so . . . independent about her,
for all she's just a country girl. I'm lost. Beyond
redemption.

Exit SOSTRATOS into the shrine.

DAUGHTER.

No. Someone's coming? If it's Father he'll murder
me.

Enter DAOS *from* GORGIAS' *house.*

DAOS.

(*talking back to someone indoors*) I've spent ages doing
the domestic chores already and he's out there
working all on his own. I've got to go. Poverty. I hate
you. What you make us put up with. You've been a
permanent guest here since heaven knows when.
210   Why don't you take a holiday?

Re-enter SOSTRATOS *with the pitcher.*

SOSTRATOS.

There you are.

DAUGHTER.

Bring it over here.

DAOS.

What's this fellow after?

SOSTRATOS.

Cheerio. Watch out for your father.

Exit DAUGHTER.

This is hell. Stop complaining, Sostratos. It's all
going to work out.

DAOS.

What's going to work out?

SOSTRATOS.

Nothing to worry about. Follow the plan. Fetch
Getas and tell him all about it.

Exit SOSTRATOS.

DAOS.

This doesn't smell right. What's going on? Very
fishy. A young chap running errands for a girl. That
220   can't be right. As for you, Knemon, God rot you for
letting an innocent young girl wander about on her

own without any sort of a chaperon. I expect this chancer found out and thought he was onto a good thing. I ought to let her brother know about this so we can arrange to keep an eye on the girl. In fact, I'd better do that right now. Look, here's a group of drunks heading for the shrine. I don't think I want to get involved with that lot.

Exit DAOS. *Enter* CHORUS.

CHORAL INTERLUDE.

ACT 2

Enter GORGIAS *and* DAOS.

GORGIAS.
Do you mean to tell me you were that casual?

DAOS.
What do you mean?

GORGIAS.
For God's sake, Daos. What you should have done if you saw this man accosting the girl was confront him and tell him he'd better not be caught at it again. Instead of passing by on the other side as though it was none of your business. She's my sister, for God's sake, and as far as you're concerned, that makes her family. Even if her father wants nothing to do with us, that's no reason for our being as bloody-minded as he is. Her scandal would be our scandal. You know what they say. 'Shame in a kindred cannot be avoided'. It's all one to the man in the street. Knock on the door.

DAOS.
Please, sir, I'd rather not. The old man scares me. If he finds me on the doorstep he'll lynch me.

GORGIAS.
He's a crotchety old devil, I grant you. You can't

230

240

250

make someone reform. There's no law against being
miserable. And there is a law saying we can't force
him to listen to reason.

DAOS.

Hang on. It's not such a wasted journey. Here he
comes again. I said he would.

GORGIAS.

The one in the posh cloak? Is that him?

DAOS.

I'm sure it is.

GORGIAS.

Shifty eyes he's got.

Enter SOSTRATOS.

SOSTRATOS.

Getas was out. Of course. Mother's off to some
260   sacrifice somewhere for some god or other – as usual
– saturating the district, so Getas is off hiring a cook.
I don't fancy getting involved with that sort of
tomfoolery so, here I am, back on the job myself.
I've had enough of these toings and froings. I'm
doing my own talking in future. Knock at the door
and over the top.

GORGIAS.

Just a moment, young man. A rather serious word in
270   your ear, if you've no objection?

SOSTRATOS.

With pleasure. Fire away.

GORGIAS.

There's a tide, you know, which knocks at every
gate, in shallows or in miseries. Success is not in
mortals to command and Fortune smiles but to a
point, young man. What plea obscures the show of
280   evil, eh? Men's evil manners live in brass while
poverty is no vice and may be mother to all virtue,
the poor man's wealth. Mark me well. In other
words, don't push your luck just because you have a

coin or two in your purse but we don't. Let deserving
be the mother of good luck.

SOSTRATOS.

Sorry? Am I meant to have done something?

GORGIAS.

It would appear to me that you are engaged in a
nefarious activity, namely attempted seduction of a   290
virgin, a free virgin at that, a crime worthy of several
death-sentences to run concurrently.

SOSTRATOS.

Good gracious.

GORGIAS.

Anyway, it is wrong that you should use your
idleness to take advantage of our lack of it. If wishes
were horses, beggars would ride. I'll tell you one
thing, though. For free. The beggar's purse may be
bottomless but prick him and he bleeds.

SOSTRATOS.

My dear chap, do let me get a word in.   300

DAOS.

Good on you, boss. You tell him.

SOSTRATOS.

Just hang on a moment and listen, will you? I saw a
girl. Here. And I fell in love with her. If that's a
crime, I'm a criminal. What can a man say? I'm not
'engaged in a nefarious activity'. I've come to talk to
her father. I'm freeborn, comfortably off and I'm
ready to take her without a dowry. And I swear to
love her always and to look after her. If I had any
evil designs upon her, or planned any sort of   310
clandestine liaison, may Pan and the Nymphs knock
me flat, here on her doorstep. I'm quite annoyed,
actually, and I don't mind telling you, that you
should think I looked like that sort of person.

GORGIAS.

Ah well. Right then. Look, if I spoke a little out of

turn, there, don't you worry about it. I'm convinced.
You've convinced me and I'm happy to declare
myself on your side. I'm not a disinterested party,
you see. I'm the girl's brother – half-brother – we
have the same mother. So. That's why I spoke as I
did. Alright? Good for you.

SOSTRATOS.

320   Good lord. So you'll give me a hand, will you?

GORGIAS.
What sort of a hand?

SOSTRATOS.
I can tell you're a decent fellow . . .

GORGIAS.
Look, I wouldn't want to invent excuses. You'd
better know the truth. The girl's father is, how can I
put it? I don't think there's anyone quite like him. I
don't think there ever has been.

SOSTRATOS.
Difficult, is he? I think I know him.

GORGIAS.
This man is the bottom line. The estate's worth, oh,
a good two talents. And he farms it single-handed
without as much as a labourer. There's no domestic
330   slave, not even a neighbour to give him a hand,
noone. His greatest joy is never to set eyes on
anybody. Except for his daughter who has to work
alongside him most of the time. She's the only one
he'll communicate with. Anyone else would be hard
pressed to get a word out of him. He says he'll only
marry her off when he finds a kindred spirit.

SOSTRATOS.
Never, you mean.

GORGIAS.
So give up, my friend. You're on a loser. For us it's
340   different. He's the penance Fate demands of family.

SOSTRATOS.
But love. Have you never been in love, a young man like you?

GORGIAS.
Hardly.

SOSTRATOS.
Why ever not? What's to stop you?

GORGIAS.
Economics, that's what. We can't afford luxuries.

SOSTRATOS.
No. You've never been in love. I can tell. That's the voice of inexperience. You warn me off? No point. Where love is concerned ' 'tis God, not Man disposes'.

GORGIAS.
Suffer, then. It's no skin off my nose. But you're wasting your time.

SOSTRATOS.
Not if I'm successful.

GORGIAS.
Which you won't be. Look. I'll come with you, if you like. He's working down in the valley at the moment, next to my land. I'll put it to him.   350

SOSTRATOS.
How exactly?

GORGIAS.
I'll bring up the question of his daughter getting married – something devoutly to be wished for in my opinion. You'll see. He'll blast off at everyone in all directions and the sort of lives they lead. I tell you, he's hardly likely to take kindly to a member of the leisured classes. You'd better keep out of sight altogether.

SOSTRATOS.
Is he there now?

GORGIAS.

He soon will be. Bound to be. He's a creature of habit.

SOSTRATOS.

360   So the girl will be with him? Is that right?

GORGIAS.

Yes. Could be.

SOSTRATOS.

Lead the way. I'm ready.

GORGIAS.

It's easy to talk.

SOSTRATOS.

Help me, will you? Please?

GORGIAS.

How can I?

SOSTRATOS.

How can you? Take me there, where you said.

GORGIAS.

Then what? Are you going to stand there in your smart cloak, watching us work?

SOSTRATOS.

Why shouldn't I?

GORGIAS.

Because he'll throw things at you and call you a lazy sod. You're going to have to do a bit of digging, that's what you're going to have to do. Alongside us. Then he might, just might, if he sees you hard at it, there's a possibility he could, maybe, listen to what you have to say because he thinks you're a country-
370   man and hard-working and poor. Perhaps.

SOSTRATOS.

Well, I'm game. Anything you say. Lead me to it.

GORGIAS.

Why punish yourself?

DAOS.

(*aside*) It'll suit me well enough if we get plenty of work out of him and he ricks his back so he can't come bothering us any longer.

SOSTRATOS.

Fetch me a spade, then.

DAOS.

You can. Have mine. There you go. I'll do a bit of dry stone walling, I think. Always something, isn't there?

SOSTRATOS.

Hand it over. My saviour.

DAOS.

I'll be off, governor. You follow on.

Exit Daos

SOSTRATOS.

The die is cast. But why the talk of dying?   380
We win the girl or lose our life in trying.

GORGIAS.

Well, good luck if you mean it.

SOSTRATOS.

Good god above. The objections you've raised at every stage have made me twice as eager. If she's been brought up in a household without women, so much the better. She'll be innocent of every vice, untouched by old wives' tales from aunts and nurses. And if her father is a trifle stern in manner, doesn't that make her the greater prize? This spade weighs a ton. It'll be the death of me. Still, mustn't   390
weaken. Stiffen the blood. Summon up the sinew. I've started and I shall persevere.

Exeunt SOSTRATOS *and* GORGIAS. *Enter* SIKON *with a sheep.*

SIKON.

This sheep. It's not your common-or-garden sheep.

It's a real beauty. Oh bugger it. If I lift it up and
carry it, the bloody thing fastens onto every passing
bush. Keep still, will you? I can't hold it. If I put it
down, it won't move. Not an inch. Contrary creature. It's given me a basting, the bastard. And I'm
meant to be the cook. Here's the shrine where
400   they're holding the sacrifice. Thank god for that.
Hail, Pan. Oy, Getas, where've you got to?

Enter GETAS *loaded down with paraphernalia.*

GETAS.
Quadruple mule-load. That's what the confounded
women have lumbered me with.

SIKON.
They're expecting an army alright. What a load of
blankets.

GETAS.
Now what?

SIKON.
Put them over there.

GETAS.
Phew. I suppose she'll have a dream about Pan of
Paiania next and we'll have to trek off over there for
a sacrifice.

SIKON.
Who's been having a dream?

GETAS.
410   Lay off, will you?

SIKON.
Getas. What dream?

GETAS.
The mistress.

SIKON.
What dream, for god's sake?

GETAS.
Ow. You're killing me. Pan . . .

SIKON.
  What Pan? This Pan?

GETAS.
  Yes, this Pan.

SIKON.
  Doing what?

GETAS.
  With her son. With Sostratos.

SIKON.
  What a nice lad.

GETAS.
  Chaining him up . . .

SIKON.
  Bloody hell!

GETAS.
  Giving him a jerkin and a spade and telling him to
  get digging for the man who lives next door here.

SIKON.
  Very peculiar.

GETAS.
  That's what the sacrifice is for. A better outcome to
  such a fearsome dream.

SIKON.
  Yes, I see. Pick up your stuff and carry it inside.
  Let's get the mattresses laid out and everything else   420
  ready. We don't want any hitches once they're here.
  God willing. And don't look so gloomy, you old
  devil. I'll see you get a decent meal anyway.

GETAS.
  You're a good cook as cooks go, I've always said so,
  but I still wouldn't trust you further than I could
  toss you.

  Exeunt SIKON *and* GETAS.

  CHORAL INTERLUDE.

ACT 3

Enter KNEMON.

KNEMON.
(*speaking backwards*) Shut the door behind me, old
woman, and bar it. Don't let anybody in, nobody,
you hear, before I get back. After dark, probably.

Enter SOSTRATOS' MOTHER, PLANGON *and
the Sacrificial Party.*

MOTHER.
430   Plangon, do hurry. We should have finished the
sacrifice by now.

KNEMON.
What mischief is this? It's a mob. Damn and blast
them.

MOTHER.
Play, Parthenis, play. Pan's tune. Never approach
Pan in silence, they say.

Enter GETAS.

GETAS.
(*to the Mother*) So you made it. Thank god for that.

KNEMON.
How revolting.

GETAS.
We've been waiting for ages.

MOTHER.
Is everything ready?

GETAS.
It certainly is. Especially the sheep. It's half dead
already. The poor thing can't wait much longer. In
440   you go. Baskets ready, ablutions, oblations. (*to
KNEMON) What are you gawping at, dumb-bell?

Exeunt the Sacrificial Party, MOTHER *and* PLAN-
GON *into the shrine.*

KNEMON.

Confound the whole confounded pack of them. I
can't get a stroke of work done. I can hardly go off
and leave the house unprotected. They're a damned
nuisance these Nymphs. I think I'll move. Knock
down the house and rebuild it somewhere else. Look
at that lot, will you. Brigands. This is meant to be a
sacrifice. They come with their sunbeds and their
bottles of wine. It's all for their benefit, nothing to do
with the gods. One pinch of incense, a crumb of
holy-cake, thanks very much, that'll do for piety. It   450
all goes on the fire, so that's good enough for the
gods. Oh, and the gods can have the extremities and
the gall-bladder, anything that humans find ined-
ible. Then they pitch in and polish off the good bits.
Open up, old woman, quickly now. I suppose I'll
have to work indoors.

Exit KNEMON. *Re-enter* GETAS.

GETAS.

Do you mean to tell me you've forgotten the pan?
You're hungover, the lot of you. So what are we
going to do about it? Bother Pan's neighbours, I
suppose.

He knocks at KNEMON*'s door*

Open up . . . Servants. I ask you. A worse set of girls
. . . Oy, anybody in? . . . Screwing's all they're fit for   460
. . . Open the door somebody . . . And lying if
anyone catches them . . . Come on. Nobody in? At
last. Someone in a hurry.

Enter KNEMON.

KNEMON.

What the hell do you think you're doing with my
door, you confounded menace?

GETAS.

No need to bite.

KNEMON.

I'll bite your bloody head off.

GETAS.

That won't be necessary, thanks everso.

KNEMON.

You're a confounded nuisance. Ever done business,
470 have we?

GETAS.

Business, no. I'm not the bailiff. I'm not serving
summonses. I just want to borrow a cooking-pot.

KNEMON.

A cooking-pot

GETAS.

Yes, a cooking-pot.

KNEMON.

You waster. Do you think I'm like you? I haven't got
cows to burn, you know.

GETAS.

Not as much as a snail, I should think. Right.
Thanks very much. Good luck to you too. Just knock
and ask. That's what the women said. So I knocked
and I asked. And you said 'No'. Right. I'll go and tell
them. God in heaven, he's a right snake, this old
480 fellow.

Exit GETAS.

KNEMON.

They'd eat you alive these people. They're animals.
They knock on your door as though you were their
best friend. Just watch the next one I catch creeping
up the path. I'll show him. I'll show the lot of them.
You see if I don't. That one's got away with it. Lucky
for him, whoever he is.

Exit KNEMON. Enter SIKON and GETAS.

SIKON.

Oh for heaven's sake, you great booby. Told you off,

did he? Maybe you asked like a shit-eater. No idea,
some people. There's a technique to it. I know. I've
done catering for thousands in town. I spend my   490
time asking neighbours for pans. All it takes is a
little finesse. If it's some old man who answers the
door, then you call him 'Father', 'Dad' even. An old
woman 'Ma'. A middle-aged woman, you show a
little respect, 'Ma'am'. If it's a young slave, it's
'There's a good lad'. You should be strung up. You
haven't a clue, have you? 'Hey, boy'. What sort of
approach is that? Compared with 'Excuse me, old
chap. Do us a favour, will you?'

GETAS *knocks at* KNEMON's *door. Enter*
KNEMON.

KNEMON.
    You back?   500

SIKON.
    What's going on, Getas?

KNEMON.
    Cross me, would you? You're doing it on purpose.
    Don't knock on my door. Didn't you hear? Old
    woman. Fetch me the whip.

SIKON.
    No. Please.

    KNEMON *grabs hold of* SIKON.

    Get off me.

KNEMON.
    Get off, eh?

SIKON.
    There's a good fellow, for God's sake.

KNEMON.
    Come back here, you.

    Exit GETAS.

SIKON.
    Lord above . . .

KNEMON.

Still got something to say, have you?

SIKON.

I only want to borrow a pan.

KNEMON.

I don't have a pan. I don't have a chopper. I don't
have any salt and I don't have any pepper. In fact I
don't have anything. And I've told everyone from
anywhere round here to keep out of my way.

SIKON.

You never told me.

KNEMON.

Then I'm telling you now.

SIKON.

510   With a vengeance. Couldn't you just see your way to
telling me where I could get one?

KNEMON.

No. I said 'no'. Got that? Anything else to witter on
about?

SIKON.

Best of luck, then.

KNEMON.

I don't need your good luck. I don't need anything.
Not from any of you.

SIKON.

Well, bad luck, then.

KNEMON.

Insufferable. They're insufferable.

Exit KNEMON.

SIKON.

I feel rotovated. 'All it takes is a little finesse'.
Sometimes. Where else can I try? If they're all so
scrap-happy round here, it won't be easy. Maybe I
520   should casserole the meat? Yes, that's the answer. A

casserole-dish I have. And bye-bye, people of Phyle.
I'll make do with what I've got.

Exit SIKON. *Enter* SOSTRATOS, *looking sun-burned.*

SOSTRATOS.
If you're looking for trouble, try Phyle. They breed it
here. God, my stomach muscles. And my back. And
neck. I ache all over. I went hard at it, being a young
fellow, digging away like an old hand, full of
enthusiasm. But in short bursts. Then I'd sort of
turn my head round so I could see if there was any   530
sign of the old man turning up with his daughter.
Then I began to feel my back. Nothing much at first.
But as time went on, I started to buckle. I was
beginning to seize up. And still nobody came. The
sun was baking. And there was Gorgias watching
me going up and down, up and down like a seesaw.
And at last he said 'I don't think he'll be coming
now, young man'. 'What are we going to do, then?' I
asked him. 'Try again tomorrow', he replied. By this   540
time Daos had arrived to take over. That was the
end of my first foray. So here I am, God alone knows
why, drawn to the place almost against my will, it
seems.

Enter GETAS.

GETAS.
(*talking backwards*) What now, blast it? I've only one
pair of hands, haven't I, not thirty? I've got the oven
going. I've fetched, I've carried. I washed up while I
was chopping the liver. I baked a cake. I've set the
table and blinded myself with the smoke. The beast   550
at the feast, that's me.

SOSTRATOS.
Hey Getas.

GETAS.
Now who wants me?

SOSTRATOS.
I do.

GETAS.
Who are you, then?

SOSTRATOS.
Are you blind?

GETAS.
Oh, Master. It's you.

SOSTRATOS.
What are you doing here?

GETAS.
You may well ask. We've finished the sacrifice and
now we're getting lunch.

SOSTRATOS.
Is my mother here?

GETAS.
She's been here ages.

SOSTRATOS.
Father?

GETAS.
Due any minute. Come on in.

SOSTRATOS.
I've a little job to do first. It's all rather convenient
this sacrifice. I'll turn up as I am and invite this
young man and his servant to come too. If we've
joined in a sacred ceremony together, they'll be
much more inclined to help me out over my marriage.

GETAS.
What was that? You want to invite somebody else to
lunch? Well, why not? You can ask three thousand
guests, as far as I'm concerned. If there's one thing
I've known all along it's that there'll be nothing for
me. And why would there be? Ask the whole world.
You've got a lovely victim there, a pleasure to

behold. Really nice these women, charm itself but what'll they offer me, eh? Not one bloody grain of salt.

570

SOSTRATOS.

Today's going to be different, Getas. Bear witness, Pan, to my generosity and don't forget I never ignore you when I pass.

Exit SOSTRATOS. *Enter* SIMICHE.

SIMICHE.

Oh disaster. Disaster. Disaster.

GETAS.

To hell with it. Here's the old man's servant.

SIMICHE.

Whatever's to become of me? I wanted to get the bucket out of the well without the master finding out it was in there in the first place, so I tied his spade onto a bit of old rope. Only that turned out to be so rotten that it broke on me . . .

580

GETAS.

Great.

SIMICHE.

And it's terrible because now the spade's down the well and so is the bucket.

GETAS.

You might as well jump in after them.

SIMICHE.

And he just happens to want to shift some dung and he can't find his spade and he's running about looking for it and shouting. Oh, there's the door. He's coming.

GETAS.

Run off, you silly old thing. Run away. He'll murder you.

Enter KNEMON.

You'll have to defend yourself now.

KNEMON.
> Where is she, the old thief?

SIMICHE.
> I didn't do it on purpose. It slipped.

KNEMON.
> Indoors. Now.

SIMICHE.
590
> What are you going to do?

KNEMON.
> Me? I'm going to lower you down, on a rope.

SIMICHE.
> No. You can't. You're a terrible man.

KNEMON.
> On the same rope, God damn it, and if it's really
> rotten, so much the better.

SIMICHE.
> I'll go and call Daos from next door.

KNEMON.
> Ruin me and shout for Daos, will you, you old
> witch? Am I not to give you orders now? Get inside
> and be quick about it.

> *Exit* SIMICHE.

> Being by yourself, it's a dreadful business. 'Never
> less alone than when alone'. Nothing else for it. I'll
> go down the well myself.

GETAS.
600
> We can let you have a grappling hook and a rope.

KNEMON.
> I'll see you in hell before I'll listen to you.

> *Exit* KNEMON.

GETAS.
> Best place for me for offering advice. There he goes
> again. Tormented old fool. What a life he leads.
> There's your typical Attic farmer. He spends his life

battling against soil that's full of rocks. What will it
grow him? A bit of thyme and sage. Nothing that's
worth anything. Here comes my master with these
guests of his. Just local labourers, by the look of
them. That's odd. Why bring them here now? And   610
how did he get to know them in the first place?

Enter SOSTRATOS, GORGIAS *and* DAOS.

SOSTRATOS.
I simply wouldn't hear of your refusing. We've
plenty of everything. Heavens, nobody turns down
an invitation to a feast after a sacrifice, do they? I
tell you, I feel as if we've been friends for ages, ages
before I even met you. Here, Daos, take your tools
in, then come and join us.

GORGIAS.
I really shouldn't leave mother by herself. See to
what she needs, Daos. I won't be long.

Exeunt severally, SOSTRATOS *and* GORGIAS *into
the shrine and* DAOS *into* GORGIAS' *house.*

   CHORAL INTERLUDE.

ACT 4

Enter SIMICHE.

SIMICHE.
Help, someone. This is terrible. Someone, help.   620

Enter SIKON

SIKON.
Lord above. Can we get on, for god's sake and pour
the bloody libations? You yell at us. You attack us.
Confound the whole household. You're mad, the lot
of you.

SIMICHE.
My master's down the well.

SIKON.
  Whatever for?

SIMICHE.
  What for? He was trying to fish out the spade and
  the bucket. And he sort of slipped and fell in.

SIKON.
  The old man? The bloody-minded one?

SIMICHE.
  Yes.

SIKON.
  Serve him right. You know what you've got to do,
630 old thing?

SIMICHE.
  What?

SIKON.
  Get a nice big stone. Or a piece of rock. And drop it
  on him.

SIMICHE.
  Please. Go down and help him.

SIKON.
  Like the man with the dog. And get bitten for my
  pains. Not bloody likely.

SIMICHE.
  Gorgias. Gorgias, where have you got to?

  Enter GORGIAS.

GORGIAS.
  Where've I got to? I'm here. Simiche, what's going
  on?

SIMICHE.
  Must I say it again? The master's in the well.

GORGIAS.
  Sostratos. Come here a minute.

  Enter SOSTRATOS.

SIMICHE.

Go on. Get a move on.

Exeunt GORGIAS, SOSTRATOS *and* SIMICHE
into KNEMON's *house.*

SIKON.

So there is justice in heaven. Thank you, God.
Refuse to lend a cooking-pot for the sacrifice, would   640
you, you old swine? Drink your well dry while you're
down there, why don't you, so you needn't offer
anyone a drop. The Nymphs have got their own
back now. Serve you right. Never mess with a cook.
Not if you know what's good for you. It's a sacred
calling, ours is. That doesn't extend to bar-staff, by
the way. What's going on? He's never dead, is he?
Who's calling 'Father'? That's a girl crying. (It must
be his daughter. No. Hang on a moment. He's not   650
dead. Too bad. Gorgias is going to spoil it. He's
found another rope. He's going down himself. And
Sostratos is going to hoist the old fool up. Yes, that's
how they'll do it. Obvious really. He'll be a fine sight
by the time he gets out. God, what will he look like?
A drowned rat.)
Brilliant. This, gentlemen, I cannot miss. By God, I
can't. And, ladies. You do your bit. Pour an extra
libation and pray that they carry out the rescue   660
execrably and disable him permanently. That'll
make him the most peaceful neighbour ever for Pan
and his party-goers. Me too, if I ever get another job
round here.

Enter SOSTRATOS.

SOSTRATOS.

By all that's holy, gentlemen, I swear to you that
nobody ever chose a better occasion to almost drown
himself. What a moment to pick. Ideal. We had no
sooner got inside than Gorgias launched himself
down the well after him. And I was up there with the   670
girl and we didn't have to do anything. I mean, what

could we do? She was tearing her hair out, of course,
and weeping and beating her breast a lot. And there
was I comforting her, the knight in shining armour –
I was, I swear I was – and saying 'There, there' and
'Never mind' and just staring at this vision. I didn't
care two hoots about the victim. Except that I had to
680   haul him out. That was a bit of a bore. Especially as
I was so busy looking at the girl, I kept letting go of
the rope. Three times, anyway. Gorgias was a
positive Atlas. He hung on like grim death and
eventually, after a great deal of effort, got him out.
And I came out here. I simply couldn't control
myself. I nearly went and kissed her. God, I'm in
love. I'm just summoning up my . . . Oh, there's the
690   door. Lord, what a sight.

Enter GORGIAS *and* KNEMON, *probably on a couch.*

GORGIAS.

Anything I can do, Knemon? Just say the word.

KNEMON.

What's there to say? I feel dreadful.

GORGIAS.

Come on. Be brave.

KNEMON.

I am being brave. He'll never be a bother to
anybody ever again, Knemon won't.

GORGIAS.

This is what comes of being a recluse, can't you see?
You all but killed yourself back there. You need
looking after at your age.

KNEMON.

I'm in a bad way. I realise that, Gorgias. Call your
mother, eh?

GORGIAS.

This minute. 'Experience is the mistress of fools'.
700   That's obvious.

Exit GORGIAS.

KNEMON.

Give me a hand, will you, girl? I want to get up.

SOSTRATOS.

Lucky man.

KNEMON.

What do you think you're standing there for? (I don't need any strangers to gloat over my misfortune. So clear off.

Re-enter GORGIAS *with* MYRRHINE.

MYRRHINE.

You look terrible. Are you alright?

KNEMON.

No, I'm not alright. You can see that.

MYRRHINE.

Then you must move to our house until you're better. You need looking after.

KNEMON.

I do need help. I have to admit it, though I hate to do so. But I have no intention of moving anywhere. I want to face death in my own way.) You won't change my mind either.

Neither you Myrrhine, nor Gorgias. You'll have to   710
make do with that.

I was wrong about one thing, I suppose. I thought I was the only person in the world who was self-sufficient. I thought that I didn't need people. Now I've stared death in the face and know he can turn up when you least expect him. My mistake and I admit it. Everyone needs a helping hand sometime. You see, I'd lost my faith in human nature. I'd watched how friendship had become no more than a commodity with a calculated profit margin. And I   720
assumed that the same was true for all relationships everywhere. It was like a physical barrier.

Now one man has shown me the error of my ways – Gorgias, with an act of pure charity towards a man

who had discouraged every knock at his door. I
never offered him the slightest assistance. I hadn't a
civil word for him, refused him as much as the time
of day. But he saved my life. A lesser man might
have said 'You spurn my approaches. Right, I'm
staying away. You've done nothing for us. I'll do
nothing for you'. And who could blame him? No,
Gorgias, let me finish. If I die as a result of this – the
way I feel at the moment I probably will – and even
730   if I don't, I want to adopt you as my son. Treat
everything of mine as yours. And I want you to look
after this girl here. Find her a husband. I couldn't do
that if I was in perfect health. Nobody would ever be
good enough for her. As for me, all I ask is that you
let me live, if I do live, the way I want to live.
Everything else, you manage. You've got your head
screwed on, thank God, and you're the obvious
guardian for your sister. Divide the property. Take
half for her dowry, and your mother and I can
740   manage on the rest. Now, help me lie down, girl.

I don't believe in wasting words, so I'll just say this.
I'd like you to understand why I am as I am. If
everyone behaved as I do, the lawcourt would be
redundant; we wouldn't need prisons; and there'd
be an end to war. Every man would be content with
his lot. Anyway, that's as maybe. So. You do as you
please. And this awkward, crusty old malcontent
will simply keep out of your way .

GORGIAS.
  Then I accept. Everything. But I'd like your assistance in finding her a husband right away, with your
  approval, that is.

KNEMON.
750   You heard my mind in this. Please. Don't bother
  me.

GORGIAS.
  There is someone who'd like a word . . .

KNEMON.

No, for heaven's sake.

GORGIAS.

To ask for her hand.

KNEMON.

No longer my business.

GORGIAS.

One of your rescuers.

KNEMON.

Who's that?

GORGIAS.

Here's the man.

KNEMON.

Come over here, you. Quite a tan. Farmer, is he?

GORGIAS.

He certainly is, Father. He's not one of your idle good-for-nothings lounging about all day.

KNEMON.

(Well, he looks fit enough. And if you approve. You see to everything.) Now have me wheeled in.

GORGIAS.

I will indeed.

Exeunt severally KNEMON *and his daughter, and* MYRRHINE.

SOSTRATOS.

So now I'm engaged to your sister.   760

GORGIAS.

Shouldn't you talk to your father?

SOSTRATOS.

Oh there'll be no problem there.

GORGIAS.

In that case, I offer you her hand in marriage, calling all the Gods to witness. There, Sostratos, all done according to form. I'm delighted to have found you so open and above-board and so prepared to commit yourself for the sake of this marriage. You're a delicate sort but you were ready to pick up a spade and do a whole day's digging. 'Wealth is best known by want', they say. That's breeding. And a man of breeding takes fortune's buffets and rewards with equal thanks. You've shown your mettle, well enough. Just see you keep it that way.

770

SOSTRATOS.

I intend to get even better. Though perhaps it isn't the thing to blow one's own trumpet. That's lucky. Here comes father now.

GORGIAS.

Kallippides? Your father's never Kallippides?

SOSTRATOS.

Yes he is.

GORGIAS.

But he's loaded, for God's sake.

SOSTRATOS.

He deserves to be. He's a damned good farmer.

Enter KALLIPPIDES.

KALLIPPIDES.

Missed lunch, I'm afraid. They'll have finished the sheep and headed for home long ago, I expect.

GORGIAS.

He's starving. Do we tell him the news?

SOSTRATOS.

After lunch. He'll be mellower than.

KALLIPPIDES.

Sostratos. What are you doing here? Have you finished eating?

SOSTRATOS.

Yes, but we've kept yours for you. Go on in.

KALLIPPIDES.

    Oh, splendid. 780

    Exit KALLIPPIDES.

GORGIAS.

    You can catch him now and talk to him, man to man.

SOSTRATOS.

    Are you going to wait indoors?

GORGIAS.

    I won't leave the house.

SOSTRATOS.

    It won't take me long. I'll come and fetch you directly.

    Exeunt severally SOSTRATOS *and* GORGIAS.

        CHORAL INTERLUDE.

ACT 5

Enter SOSTRATOS *and* KALLIPPIDES *from the shrine, and* GORGIAS *who overhears the following conversation.*

SOSTRATOS.

    But that's only half of what I'm after, Father. I was hoping for rather more than you're offering.

KALLIPPIDES.

    Whatever do you mean? I've given my consent, haven't I? You love the girl. You should marry her. I want you to. Indeed you must.

SOSTRATOS.

    I don't see it that way.

KALLIPPIDES.

    Oh, for goodness' sake. I'm acknowledging that love is a sound foundation for a young man's marriage. 790

SOSTRATOS.

What you're saying is that it's alright for me to marry that young man's sister without letting down the family. But he can't marry my sister in return. That's it, isn't it?

KALLIPPIDES.

That would never do. I don't fancy picking up a pair of impoverished in-laws. One's enough.

SOSTRATOS.

800

Money talking, as usual. I tell you, money's unreliable. If you've got it and you're sure of it, hang onto it. But if money is Fortune's gift, then why not share it? 'What Fortune gives, Fortune can withdraw'. Yes, and hand it over to someone unsuitable. So, what I'm saying, Father, is while you've got money in hand, be a bit generous, spread it about. 'Munificence is for ever'. And should you happen to hit

810

upon hard times, you'll find it an investment. Better the friend you can see than the invisible asset.

KALLIPPIDES.

Well, Sostratos, you win. I've no intention of taking my pile to the coffin. What'd be the point? It all comes to you. You want to give a friend a boost? Good luck to you. I don't need a lecture. Go ahead, Sostratos. Give it all away. Share it about. I'm convinced.

SOSTRATOS.

Really?

KALLIPPIDES.

820

Yes, really. Don't worry about it.

SOSTRATOS.

I'll just call Gorgias.

Enter GORGIAS.

GORGIAS.

I happened to catch all that. On my way out. Every

word. From the beginning. What can I say?
Sostratos, you're a true friend, really you are. But –
God, how can I put this – I wouldn't want to bite off
more than I could chew.

SOSTRATOS.

I haven't the faintest idea what you're talking about.

GORGIAS.

My sister. I'm happy to offer her to you. As your
wife. But your sister – it's very kind of you . . .

SOSTRATOS.

What do you mean kind?

GORGIAS.

I don't think I'd enjoy living off the fruits of
somebody else's labours. I need to earn my living.   830

SOSTRATOS.

What a lot of nonsense. You're not good enough for
her, is that what you're saying?

GORGIAS.

It's not a case of 'good enough'. It's what she can
offer when I have so little.

KALLIPPIDES.

Noble sentiments, damn it. But misguided.

GORGIAS.

How so?

KALIPPIDES.

Virtue as its own reward? Come now. Be swayed, as
I was.

GORGIAS.

You're right. I'd be doubly damned, still poor and
too proud to recognise a benefactor.   840

SOSTRATOS.

Excellent. All we need is the formal betrothals.

KALLIPPIDES.

Then I offer you, young man, my daughter's hand

for the provision of legitimate offspring. And as
dowry the sum of three talents.

GORGIAS.

And I can offer a talent as dowry for my sister.

KALLIPPIDES.

Can you afford that? It needn't be so much.

GORGIAS.

No, I have that.

KALLIPPIDES.

You don't want to split up the farm, Gorgias. Now
go and fetch your mother and your sister and bring
them over to meet my women.

GORGIAS.

Right.

SOSTRATOS.

850   We can all stay here for the party tonight and hold
the weddings tomorrow. Gorgias, fetch the old man.
He'll be better looked after with us.

GORGIAS.

He won't want to come, Sostratos.

SOSTRATOS.

Twist his arm.

GORGIAS.

I can but try.

SOSTRATOS.

We'll have a great booze-up, Dad. The women too,
up all night.

KALLIPPIDES.

Quite the reverse. The women will do the boozing
and it's us who'll be up all night. I'll go and get
860   things organised.

Exit KALLIPPIDES.

SOSTRATOS.

You do that. Never give up. That's the moral. Faint

heart never won what's gained by honest toil. And I'm the living witness. In a single day, contrary to all expectation, I've achieved the marriage of my dreams.

Enter GORGIAS with his mother and sister.

GORGIAS.
Get a move on, do.

SOSTRATOS.
This way, ladies. Mother, they're here. No Knemon?

The women enter the shrine.

GORGIAS.
He kept asking me to invite old Simiche too, so he'd be left in peace.

SOSTRATOS.
A lost cause, that one.

870

GORGIAS.
That's Knemon.

SOSTRATOS.
Well, too bad. Let's go.

GORGIAS.
Just a minute, Sostratos. Those women in there. I feel embarrassed.

SOSTRATOS.
Oh fiddlesticks. In you go. Just think of them as family.

Exeunt SOSTRATOS and GORGIAS. Enter SIMICHE.

SIMICHE.
I'm off too, I swear I am.

Enter GETAS.

You can just lie there. By yourself, you miserable old . . . It was a civil invitation, for heaven's sake. And you turn it down. You'll come to a bad end, you will,

damned if you don't. Worse than now. And good
luck to you.

GETAS.

I'll go and see how he is.

Music (a stage direction in the original manuscript).

880   Don't start playing yet, you stupid man. We're not
ready. I've still got that old invalid to sort out. Hold
it.

SIMICHE.

Somebody else can go and sit with him for once. I'm
losing my mistress. All I want is a few words with
her, a chance to tell her a few things and wish her
luck.

GETAS.

That makes sense. Off you go then. I'll hold the fort.

Exit SIMICHE.

Just the chance I've been looking for. I'll show the
old devil. No fear of interruption. They're all too
busy drinking. Hey, Cook. Sikon. Get yourself out
890   here a minute. This should be fun.

Enter SIKON.

SIKON.

Someone call?

GETAS.

Me. What would you say to the chance of getting
your own back for being fucked about back there?

SIKON.

Fucked about? What are you on about?

GETAS.

The old man, the bloody-minded one. He's in there
by himself, fast asleep.

SIKON.

Is he alright?

GETAS.

Could be worse.

SIKON.

Is he strong enough to get up and hit us?

GETAS.

I don't think he's strong enough to get up at all.

SIKON.

What a nice idea. I'll go and ask to borrow something. He'll go spare.

GETAS.

That would be good. What if we fetched him out here first, then started banging on his door? That'll really annoy him. What a laugh.   900

SIKON.

I'm scared of Gorgias. I don't want him catching us.

GETAS.

They're all drinking. There's far too much noise. No one'll notice. We'll teach him a few manners. He is part of the family now and if he carries on like this he'll be insufferable.

SIKON.

Yes. Why not?

GETAS.

Just be careful when you bring him out. Off you go then.

SIKON.

Hang on a moment. And don't you disappear either.

SIKON *exits into* KNEMON's *house and wheels him out.*

GETAS.

Keep quiet, for God's sake.

SIKON.

I am bloody keeping quiet.

GETAS.

Right a bit.

SIKON.
> There.

GETAS.
> That'll do. Now. The moment has arrived. I'll lead
> off.

To the musician.

910   Take your tempo from me.

GETAS *starts to bang on the door.*

SIKON.
> Hey there, boy. Hey lads. Good lads.
> Boys. Hey boys.

KNEMON.
> Ahhh. Murder!

SIKON.
> Lads. Good lads. Come on. Come on, boys.

KNEMON.
> Ahhh. Murder!

SIKON.
> Who's this then? You belong here, do you?

KNEMON.
> Of course I do. What do you want?

SIKON.
> Pans. I want to borrow some. And pots.

KNEMON.
> Give me a hand up, someone.

SIKON.
> You've got them. I know you have. And seven
> trestles. Twelve tables. Tell them inside the rest, will
> you, lads? Must rush.

KNEMON.
> I have none of this.

SIKON.
> None of it?

KNEMON.
How many times do you need telling?

SIKON.
Well, I can't hang about.

KNEMON.
This is frightful. How did I get out here? What am I
doing outside?   920

SIKON.
Your turn.

GETAS.
Hey there, boy. Hey girls. Hey fellows.
Boy. Hey, porter.

KNEMON.
Are you raving mad? You'll smash the door down.

GETAS.
We could use twelve rugs.

KNEMON.
Where from?

GETAS.
And let us have a screen-curtain, would you, a nice
big one, a hundred foot long. It must be foreign, and
embroidered.

KNEMON.
It's a whip I could do with. Old woman. Where's the
old woman got to?

GETAS.
I'll try the other door, shall I?

KNEMON.
Just clear off out of it. Simiche! Where are you,
woman? Damn and blast the whole bloody lot of
you. What do you want?

SIKON.
(*returning to the fray*) A wine bowl. I need a big,
bronze wine-bowl.

KNEMON.
Won't anyone give me a hand up?

GETAS.
930   You've got a curtain, haven't you? You have, you
old so-and-so, you know you have.

KNEMON.
I have not, for God's sake.

SIKON.
And no wine-bowl?

KNEMON.
I'll kill that Simiche.

SIKON.
Now, sit down. And shut up. And listen.

You shun company, despise women, turn down an
invitation to a sacrifice. Right. Then this is your
penance and there's nobody around to help you out.
So button up and put up with it. And listen while I
tell you what happened in there.

Music.

These women in your life
Met with warmth and affection.
Your wife and your daughter
Charmed all they encountered.
Besides there was food, a wonderful spread,
940   And convivial drinking for everyone present.

Still listening? Don't fall asleep on me.

GETAS.
No. Don't.

KNEMON.
This is terrible.

SIKON.
What's so terrible? Do you not want to be a part
of all that? Let me tell the rest of it.

Everyone lively
Everywhere excitement.

I set the tables
And I spread the couches.
Now do you know me? It's me. I'm the cook.
The cook. Are you listening? And this is my job.

GETAS.
And a gentleman too.

SIKON.
One poured the noble vintage into the rounded
    bowl,
Mixing in soft spring water nurtured by the
    Nymphs.
One charged the men's glasses, another the
    women's.
Watering the sand, if you follow my meaning.
Then one of the maids, who was just a touch
    tipsy,
The bonniest of girls even with her face veiled,   950
Started to dance, a little self-conscious,
But delicately, decorously, lovely to watch.
Till a friend took her hand and picked up her
    rhythm
Swaying, gyrating, sharing her motion.

GETAS.
Your suffering's behind you, severe as it was. Now
    come and dance. Up you get.

KNEMON.
Confound the pair of you. What do you want?

GETAS.
Up you get. You are awkward.

KNEMON.
Stop it, for God's sake.

GETAS.
Let us take you in.

KNEMON.
What am I to do?

GETAS.

Dance, that's what.

KNEMON.

Oh, very well. I'll endure it somehow, I suppose.

GETAS.

Congratulations. We win. Well done us. Donax,
Sikon, Syrus, come on, lads. Lift him and carry
him in.

Enter attendants.

And as for you, the next time we catch you causing
trouble, you won't get off so lightly. And don't you
forget it. Garlands someone. Fetch the torches.

These are distributed.

SIKON.

One for you.

Exeunt SIKON, KNEMON *and attendants into the
shrine.*

GETAS.

There, then. That's that.

Now audience, boys and youths and men of more
    maturity,

You've witnessed our encounters with this
    malcontent.

Contentedly, we hope, you've seen our victory.

And if content, applaud our antics now.

Crowning our day with Victory's accolade.

END

960

MENANDER

THE WOMAN FROM SAMOS

translated by J. Michael Walton

Characters

MOSCHION, adopted son of Demeas
CHRYSIS, the woman from Samos
PARMENON, Demeas' slave
DEMEAS, a well-to-do Athenian
NIKERATOS, Demeas' neighbour
A COOK
PLANGON (non-speaking), Nikeratos' daughter
MYRRHINE (non-speaking), Nikeratos' wife
ATTENDANTS
CHORUS (indicated in the text only by a stage-
    direction)

Some of Menander's text from the early part of the play is missing. To provide the continuity of a complete piece, the present translator has filled in the gaps with invented material of about the right length. All such material appears in brackets.

ACT 1

Athens. The adjacent houses of DEMEAS *and* NIKERA-TOS. *Enter* MOSCHION.

MOSCHION.

(Heavens, what a business. What on earth am I going to do? After all, it's not really my fault. Well it is, but everything's become rather complicated. Her father won't be happy, that's for sure. Nor will mine, if it comes to that, however long the pair of them are away. Yes, it's my father Demeas who'll be the real problem. Not being my natural father he's more strict than if he were. You see, my own father died when I was a baby and I never knew my mother either. Demeas adopted me, though he's a bachelor, and brought me up as his own son. I'd do anything rather than upset him.)

But what's there to get upset about? It's regrettable, yes. I was in the wrong, I admit it. Look. Gentlemen. I think it would be best if I were to tell you the whole story, beginning with the sort of man my adoptive father is.

I look back on my childhood as comfortable. Nothing more to say except that at the time I didn't realise how comfortable. At eighteen I was registered as a citizen in the ordinary way, 'nem con' as they say, though between ourselves my origins are somewhat humble, God knows. Comfortable! Now look at me. My situation could hardly be more uncomfortable.

10

As a theatre patron I could afford to make a bit of
a splash, if I say so myself, and in charity work too.
Demeas kept hounds for me, horses – in the services
I held a distinguished cavalry commission. A friend
in need could always turn to me. Thanks to my
father, I was a man. And I did thank him, by always
behaving in public as a gentleman. Then it happened. Well, I might as well make all our affairs
20   public. I'm not in any hurry.

There was this woman, you see, from Samos,
called Chrysis, not a citizen so she was a courtesan.
Demeas fell in love with her: that's human nature,
after all. But he tried to conceal it, from shame,
perhaps, I don't know. He certainly didn't want me
to find out, but I did. I reckoned that if he was going
to keep younger rivals at bay, she would have to
become his full-time mistress. As I say, he wasn't
keen on that, probably because he thought he would
30   be setting me a bad example.

(He's a man of principle, you see but, like most
men of principle, he's a stickler for keeping up
appearances. His pride is important to him and I
couldn't admit to knowing about the woman.
Instead, I confided in our neighbour Nikeratos, who
lives here next door with his wife Myrrhine and his
daughter Plangon. Nikeratos has always been as
poor as my father's rich but he's not afraid to speak
his mind. And Plangon . . . but more of her in a
minute. Nikeratos confronted Demeas and told him
that he'd been seen with this Samian woman and
how they'd seemed fond of one another. And what
with one thing and another and Demeas being a
bachelor, why not invite Chrysis to share his house
with him. They couldn't marry, of course, that's the
law, but there are no laws against being happy.

Finally Demeas agreed, on condition, as he told
Nikeratos and Chrysis, that there could be no

question of children because any child would be
illegitimate. And anyway, I was his sole heir. He
asked my blessimng too which I willingly gave,
though I had to pretend that the whole affair was a
great surprise to me.

For a few months all went well. Then Demeas was
called abroad on business. Rather than travel alone
he invited Nikeratos to accompany him. He was sad
to leave Chrysis but at least he knew she was safe in
his house. Tearful farewells all round. Then, the day
before they're due to leave, what happened? Chrysis
announced she was pregnant. True to his word and,
love her or not, Demeas' parting words were, 'Get
rid of it or else'.

Are you with me so far? Father abroad. Mistress
pregnant with a child she can't keep. Nikeratos also
abroad leaving behind his daughter Plangon. Now
Plangon's a beautiful girl, but in an awkward
position because Nikeratos can't afford to give her a
dowry.)

With the two men away, Plangon's mother
became close friends with my father's mistress,
Chrysis. In and out of one another's houses all the
time. One day I happened to come back unexpec-
tedly from the estate to find Plangon and Myrrhine
with a lot of other women at our house celebrating
the Adonis festival. There was lots of eating and
drinking and fun and games – you know how it is –
and because I'd just come home, I couldn't resist
going to have a look. I wouldn't have been able to
sleep anyway with the racket they were making. The
roof was decorated with fruit and flowers and the
women were up there in ones and twos dancing the
night away.

I'm not sure I want to tell you what happened
next. Quite disgraceful, of course. But it's a bit late
to worry about that. Still, I admit I am ashamed of
myself. The girl got pregnant. There, I've told you

40

50   the result. You can fill in the bit in between yourself.
        I don't deny it. It was all my fault and I went
        straight to Plangon's mother and swore to marry the
        girl as soon as her father returned home with my
        father. The baby was born recently and I brought it
        to our house. As it happened – a fortunate coincid-
        ence really – Chrysis had given birth to her child
        (only a week or two earlier but that baby died. She
        knew that Demeas had wanted her to get rid of it but
        she had hoped somehow that, once he had seen the
        baby and once he had seen her again, she would be
        able to win him round to letting her keep it. The
        question never arose but, having so recently lost a
        baby of her own, Chrysis agreed to act as wet-nurse
        to Plangon's. This way noone outside the family
        would know of Plangon's disgrace until, that is, her
        father returned from abroad. Then Plangon and I
        could get married and take the child back as our
        own.

            So far so good. The problem will be with my
        father who won't be happy about me marrying a girl
        without a dowry. And if he catches sight of Chrysis
        with a baby he thinks is hers, there's no knowing
        how he'll react.

            Now Parmenon tells me that father's ship has
        been sighted and should be landing today. I sent
        him off to the harbour for news but, whatever
        happens, I'm expecting a rough passage. Father's
        bound to think I've let him down. And after all that
        he's done for me. I think I'd better head down there
        myself and see what the slave's found out.

        Exit MOSCHION. *Enter* CHRYSIS.

    CHRYSIS.
        What a sweet child. I could almost believe he is
        mine. I'm still not sure if we're doing the right thing.
        Demeas is a dear man and he's been good to me, but
        he'll have to know the truth sometime. I don't know

how he'll take it. He's so strait-laced. And he does
have a temper. If we can win him round to
Moschion marrying Plangon, then he's bound to
accept that all Moschion did was anticipate his
wishes a little. Isn't he? And if the worst comes to the
worst, I can always continue to say the child is mine,
whatever he said before he left. But then, what about
Plangon? I don't know. I wonder what the news will
be from the harbour.)

    Oh, here they come and in a hurry. I'll hang on
and listen to what they have to say.

Enter MOSCHION *and* PARMENON.

MOSCHION.
Did you actually see father, Parmenon?

PARMENON.
I told you. You don't listen, do you?

MOSCHION.
Nikeratos with him?

PARMENON.
They're both here.

MOSCHION.
That's something to be thankful for, I suppose.

PARMENON.
Be a man, can't you? All you have to do is tell them
about the marriage the moment you see them.

MOSCHION.
How can I? Now it's staring me in the face, I've lost
my nerve.

PARMENON.
What are you talking about?

MOSCHION.
I can't face my father. I'm too ashamed.

PARMENON.
Think of the girl you wronged. And her mother. You
great softy, you're trembling like a leaf.

60

CHRYSIS.

Why are you shouting at him, you silly man?

PARMENON.

70   Is that you, Chrysis? You want to know why I'm
shouting at him? That's funny, that is. I'll tell you
what I'm shouting about. I want there to be a
marriage, right? I want this . . . this . . . I want him
to stop blubbing all over the porch. And I want him
to start remembering that he swore an oath: sacrifices, garlands, wedding-cake. He's trying to wriggle
out of it. Now, have I got something to shout about?

MOSCHION.

I'll do it. Everything. What have I got to say?

CHRYSIS.

There, there. Of course you will

MOSCHION.

The baby belongs to Chrysis and she's bringing it up
because it's hers. That's it, right?

CHRYSIS.

Yes, why not?

MOSCHION.

Father's going to be so angry.

CHRYSIS.

80   And after a while he'll stop being angry. Why?
Because, my dear, he loves me. He's a man in love
and he can't help himself, any more than you can.
'Love hath the better of temper'. There. Besides I'd
put up with anything rather than see the poor mite
in some slum foster-home.

(MOSCHION.

What about Plangon?

CHRYSIS.

Plangon can bide her time. As she doesn't have the
baby, she needn't tell her father anything until
you've seen him and confessed.

MOSCHION.

He'll be furious too.

CHRYSIS.

Not when he hears you're asking for her hand.
Particularly if you ask to marry her before you tell
him she's already had your baby. Besides, he's a
poor man. He should be glad to get her off his hands.

MOSCHION.

That's the other problem.

PARMENON.

What is?

MOSCHION.

My father. He'll never agree to my marrying someone without a dowry. You know what he's like about
money.

CHRYSIS.

He couldn't have been more generous to you. He
knows Nikeratos and he respects him. They've been
travelling companions for the best part of a year.
He's not going to turn round and forbid you to
marry Plangon on financial grounds. Especially
when you've already fathered a child on her.

MOSCHION.

I'll never be able to tell him that. I won't have the
nerve. He'll be furious.

CHRYSIS.

There'll be nothing for him to be furious about until
it's too late. For the present, the baby's mine and if
he's going to be furious with anyone, he'll be furious
with me. Parmenon, come inside. If they've docked
already we need to get ready. He could be here any
time.

Exeunt CHRYSIS *and* PARMENON.

MOSCHION.

I'm in such a muddle. Who do I tell about what

baby? And when? I'm going to make a terrible mess
of everything and everyone will be cross with me. I
wish we'd never started this.)

What if I went and hanged myself? If only I was
90　better at talking to people. Perhaps I'll go off
somewhere quiet and rehearse what I'm going to
say. 'What can't be cured must be endured'. I'll have
to make the best of it.

Exit MOSCHION. *Enter* DEMEAS *and* NIKERA-
TOS *with slaves and luggage.*

DEMEAS.
What did I tell you? It's fine to be back. You can feel
the difference. After that frightful place.

NIKERATOS.
The Black Sea. What's it add up to? Stupid old men;
endless fish; unrewarding business. As for Byzan-
100　tium, a nasty taste in the mouth. And that's it. But
back home, Lord, everyone as honest as the day is
long. A poor man's paradise.

DEMEAS.
Dear old Athens. Blessings upon you. I wish you
everything you deserve. We who love our city are the
most fortunate people in the world. Oy, you (*to
slaves*). Get inside. Don't stand there gawping.
What's the matter with you?

NIKERATOS.
You know what I could never get used to, Demeas?
The sun. Most of the time you never saw it.
Everything shrouded in fog.

DEMEAS.
110　There was nothing worth looking at. That's how
they manage with so little illumination.

NIKERATOS.
God knows, you're right there.

DEMEAS.
Our problem no longer. Now. That other little

matter we were talking about. What do you want to
do?

NIKERATOS.
Marrying my daughter to your boy, you mean?

DEMEAS.
Yes.

NIKERATOS.
I still feel the same. Let's take the bull by the horns
and name the day.

DEMEAS.
You really think so?

NIKERATOS.
Absolutely.

DEMEAS.
Splendid. It's what I've been hoping for all along.

NIKERATOS.
Give me a call when you're thinking of going out.

Exit NIKERATOS.

(DEMEAS.
What a match. He's such a proud man, I thought he
wouldn't agree. That's one of the reasons I took him
away with me. So he could see that as far as I'm
concerned money is not that important. Poor Nikeratos. So worried that he'd never find a husband for
Plangon because he couldn't afford a dowry. Why
should I care? He's a good man. She's a nice enough
girl. Moschion's all I have. Even if he's not my flesh
and blood, he's never wanted for anything and he
won't now. Who cares about a dowry? As long as
Nikeratos agrees to sign over everything he has to
Moschion the moment he dies, that's good enough
for me. But how do I break it to Moschion? He's a
conventional sort of boy. Likes to go about things in
the proper way. I wouldn't wish to upset him. I'm
not sure he ever accepted Chrysis. I know he said he

did but he was a bit funny about it. I've missed her
so much in the last months. I can't put it off any
longer. I have to go in and see her. Do excuse me but
there's a group of dancers coming up the street.
They'll keep you entertained till I get back.

Exit DEMEAS.

CHORAL INTERLUDE.

ACT 2

Enter DEMEAS.

DEMEAS.

That does it. That's it. What was the first thing I
said to her when she entered my house? 'No children'. What was the last thing I said before I left and
she told me she was pregnant? 'Get rid of it'. And she
agreed. She agreed. What do I find? I come home
after months abroad and what's the first thing I see?
Chrysis, nursing a baby. Would you credit it? Why,
here's Moschion. He looks distracted about something.

Enter MOSCHION.

MOSCHION.

120   I got all the way out of the city, sat down to plan
what I was going to say and started daydreaming,
planning the wedding instead. I made the sacrifices,
sent invitations to the wedding-breakfast, ordered
the libations. Then I cut the cake and started to hum
the wedding-song. Silly of me. When I'd had enough
of that . . . goodness, there's father. I hope he didn't
hear what I've been saying. Father. Welcome back.

DEMEAS.

Moschion, my boy. I'm overjoyed to see you.

MOSCHION.

You don't look overjoyed. Whatever's the matter?

DEMEAS.

The matter? Only that I hadn't realised my mistress
thinks she's my wife. 130

MOSCHION.

Thinks she's your wife? How could she? What are
you talking about?

DEMEAS.

Apparently she's had a baby, my baby. To hell with
the both of them. She can clear out and take the
bastard with her.

MOSCHION.

You can't do that.

DEMEAS.

Can't I just? What do you expect me to do? Bring up
a child that's illegitimate? Not my style. Oh no, not
my style at all.

MOSCHION.

Illegitimate? Who's legitimate, for God's sake? Any
man born might be illegitimate.

DEMEAS.

It's just a joke to you, isn't it?

MOSCHION.

I'm perfectly serious, I swear it. I can see no 140
destinction between being of one race or of another.
To anyone who believes in justice, if a man's good,
he's legitimate and if he's bad, he's a bastard.

(You always claim to do what's right and proper,
but how do you know what is right and proper? Is it
right and proper to throw Chrysis out of your house
for having a baby when you love her and she loves
you?

DEMEAS.

I gave strict instructions . . .

MOSCHION.

Would you marry her if you could?

DEMEAS.

The question doesn't arise.

MOSCHION.

But would you? Because, if so, the child is as good as legitimate.

DEMEAS.

Perhaps I'm being too hasty. Not that I agree with you, mind.

MOSCHION.

Then you won't tell her to leave and she can keep the baby?

DEMEAS.

I'll think about it. But, in return, there's something you can do for me

MOSCHION.

Anything you want, Father. You know that.

DEMEAS.

I've been giving the matter some thought and it seems to me it's time you got married.

MOSCHION.

Married?

DEMEAS.

I never did. And look at the result. I find myself in the position of being a father when I can't be a father.

MOSCHION.

But I don't want to get married. Or rather I do want to get married.

DEMEAS.

I've found the ideal girl for you. Of course, she's not entirely ideal.

MOSCHION.

Who do you have in mind?

DEMEAS.

Nikeratos' daughter, Plangon.

MOSCHION.

Plangon?

DEMEAS.

Oh, I know it takes a little getting used to. She hasn't got a dowry. But Nikeratos has agreed that he will bequeath his entire estate to you. He's older than I am so you shouldn't have to wait that long. I've got to know him well over the past few months. He's not clever, of course, and he's never made any money but he's a decent sort of a fellow.

MOSCHION.

Yes.

DEMEAS.

And she's a nice girl. Quite pretty really.

MOSCHION.

This is wonderful. You see, I already want to marry her. We've been waiting for you and Nikeratos to get back to ask for your permission.

DEMEAS.

You mean it?

MOSCHION.

I'm in love with her. I'm in love with Plangon. And we want the wedding to be as soon as possible.)

DEMEAS.

My boy. Why, that's splendid.

(MOSCHION.

There is a slight complication.)

DEMEAS.

Yes, of course. But if they're prepared to offer her, you're prepared to accept.   150

MOSCHION.

No question. You can see I'm serious, can't you?

DEMEAS.

You mean it? No question? Moschion, I understand. I can see what you're telling me. I'll be off to

have a word with Nikeratos. This minute. To tell
him to get going.

MOSCHION.

We've already got everything ready. I'll go indoors
and have a wash and offer a libation. Then I'll go
and fetch the girl.

DEMEAS.

160 Wait till I find Nikeratos. I have to check that he's
still happy.

MOSCHION.

He's bound to agree. I'll leave you. I'd just be in the
way.

Exit MOSCHION.

DEMEAS.

Well, well. 'There's a divinity that shapes our ends',
as they say, 'untalk'd of and unseen'. I never even
knew he was in love.

(But then a lot can happen in nine months. What
a splendid fellow he's turned out to be. So frank, so
artless. The way he stood up to me over Chrysis and
the baby. There's not an ounce of guile in him. And
fearless with it. I have to confess that when Nikeratos first suggested the match I wasn't keen. But
everything's worked out for the best. Ah, here he
comes.

Enter NIKERATOS.

Not a moment to lose, Nikeratos. Everything under
control? Good. Make haste. The wedding is on and
today.

NIKERATOS.

170 What wedding?

DEMEAS.

Moschion's, of course.

NIKERATOS.

To whom?

DEMEAS.
To your daughter. To Plangon.

NIKERATOS.
Oh, I'm not sure about that.

DEMEAS.
Not sure? It's all settled. We agreed.

NIKERATOS.
Her mother mightn't agree, though. Then there's
Plangon.

DEMEAS.
What have they got to do with it? Don't you see?
Moschion's in love with her. He told me so himself.
If he wants to marry Plangon and we want him to
marry Plangon, who else comes into it?

NIKERATOS.
It's Myrrhine. After you'd said what you said and I
agreed with what you said, I went straight in and
told Myrrhine that I'd found Plangon a husband.

DEMEAS.
Well?

NIKERATOS.
She gave me a funny look.

DEMEAS.
Is that it?

NIKERATOS.
And then she said 'What's the hurry?'

DEMEAS.
So what did you say?

NIKERATOS.
I went and told Plangon.

DEMEAS.
And what did Plangon say?

NIKERATOS.
She didn't say anything. Just burst into tears and
ran off.

DEMEAS.

180   What's wrong with Moschion, for heaven's sake? A finer boy never lived.

NIKERATOS.

No, of course. I quite agree with you. Only they don't know that it's Moschion.

DEMEAS.

Why don't they know?

NIKERATOS.

I forgot to tell them. I just said I'd found her a husband. It was the idea of husband that seemed to upset them, not the idea of Moschion.

DEMEAS.

We can't be doing with this sort of nonsense. You approve of Moschion, don't you? Of course you do. Anybody would. The whole thing's ridiculous. So the wedding can be today. Agreed?

NIKERATOS.

I'm not at all sure. Wouldn't it be more sensible . . .?

DEMEAS.

The sooner the better. If we're going to fix a day, what's wrong with today?

NIKERATOS.

There's a great deal to do.

DEMEAS.

I don't believe in hanging about. Particularly if the women are shilly-shallying. Parmenon. We're having a wedding. Where is that slave?

Enter PARMENON.)

190   Parmenon. Bouquets. Sacrificial victims. Sesame-seed cake. Off to the market and don't come back till you've bought everything.

PARMENON.

Everything? Right, master. Leave it to me.

DEMEAS.

Get a move on. This minute. And bring back a cook.

PARMENON.

Bring back cook. Buy everything else.

DEMEAS.

Yes, yes. Buy everything.

PARMENON.

I'll run and fetch some money.

Exit PARMENON.

DEMEAS.

Still here, Nikeratos?

NIKERATOS.

I'd better go in and tell my wife to make preparations. Then I'll follow him down to the market.

Exit NIKERATOS. *Re-enter* PARMENON.

PARMENON.

Don't ask me. I don't know anything except that I've
got my orders and I'm doing what I'm told.

DEMEAS.

He won't find it easy convincing his wife, that's for   200
sure. You should never waste time explaining things
to people. Parmenon. Don't hover, boy. Off you go.
At the double.

Exit PARMENON.

(Why do people do it? Why do they let wives get
away with it? As soon as a man decides on something, his wife dreams up a reason why not. He'd be
much better off not telling her in the first place. Or
be like me and not get married at all.

Enter NIKERATOS.

DEMEAS.

Well?

NIKERATOS.

I went in and told them that she was going to marry
Moschion whether she liked it or not.

DEMEAS.
  More tears?

NIKERATOS.
  Not a bit of it. Smiles all round. I'll never understand them.

DEMEAS.
  That's a relief. I'll go and see how Moschion's
  getting on and you'd better go back in before they
  change their minds.

  Exeunt DEMEAS *and* NIKERATOS *to their own
  houses.*

  CHORAL INTERLUDE.

  ACT 3

Enter DEMEAS.

DEMEAS.
  I'm flabberghasted. Speechless.)
  It was all plain sailing. Everything going swim-
  mingly when, out of nowhere, a tornado. Smashes
  over the unsuspecting crew and sinks them without
210   trace. That's me. There I was helping with the
  wedding preparations, sacrificing to the gods, all
  according to plan. Now, God in Heaven, I don't
  know if I can believe my eyes. Here and now I
  parade myself before you as an unequivocal booby.
  Would you believe it? Look at me. Am I in my right
  mind or out of it? Or beating my head with the
  wrong end of the stick?
  What happened was this. I went indoors, quick as
  I could, to get on with the wedding preparations.
  Lined up all the slaves. Gave them their orders
  perfectly clearly, cleaning, cooking, getting the
220   baskets ready. Everything was under control,

though there was a certain amount of confusion with
all the running about. Only natural. Someone had
put the baby down on a couch where it wouldn't be
in the way. Of course, it was yelling. And the women
were all shouting at once 'Flour. Water over here.
Fetch the olive-oil. More charcoal'. I joined in to
give them a hand. Which is how I found myself in
the store-cupboard. I was quite a while in there,
sorting things out and seeing what was what.   230

While I was in there this woman came downstairs
into the room next to the store-cupboard. That's
where the loom is kept and you have to go through it
to get upstairs or to the store-cupboard. It was
Moschion's nurse, quite elderly now and a freewo-
man though she used to be a slave. Seeing the baby
left to cry and nobody looking after it, and not
realising that I was in the store-room, she saw no   240
reason to guard her tongue. She went up to the baby
and said the sort of things they say to babies. 'Nice
baby. What a good boy'. That sort of thing. 'Where's
your mummy, then?' Then she picked it up and gave
it a cuddle. So it stopped crying and she said to it
'Oh dear, oh dear. It doesn't seem yesterday I was
nursing Moschion – you've got his eyes alright – now
he's got a boy of his own (and nobody can be
bothered with you, poor thing'. And more in the
same vein.) until some slip of a girl came rushing in.   250
'Here, the child needs changing', declares the old
woman. 'What's the matter with you? You can't
neglect a baby just because its father's getting
married.' Immediately the girl hushes her up. 'Keep
your voice down, idiot. *He's* in there.' 'He's not is he?
Where?' 'In the store-cupboard.' Then she says
loudly 'The mistress is calling for you, Nurse. Run
along, now.' And not so loudly, 'He won't have
heard. Don't worry.' 'Me and my mouth', the old   260
woman mutters and off she trots, Lord knows where.

Out I came. I was calm. I was collected, as you

see I am now, just as though I hadn't heard a word
and hadn't begun to wonder if . . . First thing I clap
eyes on is my Samian with the baby, breast-feeding.
The baby must be hers. That's obvious. But who's
the father?. It's mine. It must be mine. The alterna-
tive . . . well, frankly, I'm not prepared to put it into
270   words because I don't believe it. All I have done is
present the evidence. I heard what I heard. I'm not
upset. Not at all. Not yet. I know my boy, indeed I
do. He's a gentleman, always has been, and respect
for me . . . absolutely. The only thing is that I did
overhear that nurse. And she was his nurse once.
And she didn't know I was there. And looking back
at how fond of the baby Chrysis is, and how she
persuaded me, against my better judgement, to keep
it . . . I'm altogether furious.

280   That's handy. Here's Parmenon back from
market with the hired help. I'll let him take them
indoors.

Enter PARMENON, COOK *and assistants.*

PARMENON.
God almighty, Cook. I don't know why you bother
with cooking knives. You could mince anything with
that tongue of yours.

COOK.
You don't know what you're talking about.

PARMENON.
Don't I?

COOK.
No, you don't. That's what I think. What if I need to
know how many tables you're going to use, how
many waitresses, the serving-time, what to do about
290   a *maitre d'*, have you enough crockery, is it an
outdoor kitchen? And there's another thing . . .

PARMENON.
Chop, chop, chop. You're mincing me again.

COOK.
The hell with you.

PARMENON.
After you. You lot, get indoors.

Exeunt COOK *and attendants.*

DEMEAS.
Parmenon.

PARMENON.
Someone call my name?

DEMEAS.
Yes, me.

PARMENON.
Oh master, there you are. Well, cheerio.

DEMEAS.
Get rid of your basket and come back here.

PARMENON.
Right you are. Happy to oblige.

Exit PARMENON.

DEMEAS.
Never misses a trick, this chap, I'm sure of that. He
knows what's going on round here if anybody does.   300
There's the door. He's coming.

Re-enter PARMENON.

PARMENON.
That's it, Chrysis. Everything the cook wants,
but for God's sake, keep the old woman away from
the dishes. Right, master, what can I do for you?

DEMEAS.
You can come over here for a start, away from the
door. A bit further.

PARMENON.
Anything you say.

DEMEAS.
Now listen here, Parmenon. I swear to you, I do

really, that I don't particularly want to give you a
thrashing.

PARMENON.

A thrashing? What did I do?

DEMEAS.

You're hiding something, I know you are.

PARMENON.

Me? What? No. I'm not. I swear I'm not. By
anything you like, Dionysus, Apollo, Zeus, Ascle-
310   pius . . .

DEMEAS.

That'll do. No need for any swearing. I'm telling
you.

PARMENON.

Never in . . .

DEMEAS.

Just look. Over there.

PARMENON.

Right. I'm looking.

DEMEAS.

That child. Whose is it?

PARMENON.

Mmmm. Child.

DEMEAS.

I'll ask you once more. Whose is that baby?

PARMENON.

Ah, that baby. That's Chrysis'.

DEMEAS.

And who is the father?

PARMENON.

You are. According to her.

DEMEAS.

Now you are in trouble. Make a fool of me, would
you?

PARMENON.
What did I do?

DEMEAS.
I know everything. I know the baby is Moschion's
and I know that you know, and that it's for him that
she's bringing it up.

PARMENON.
Who says so?

DEMEAS.
Everybody says so. Now, answer me. Am I right?

PARMENON.
Well, yes, master, but we didn't want it becoming   320
common knowledge.

DEMEAS.
Common knowledge? Slaves. Where are you? Fetch
me a whip, one of you, for this reprobate.

PARMENON.
No, please.

DEMEAS.
I'll mark you for life.

PARMENON.
Mark me?

DEMEAS.
Here and now.

PARMENON.
I really have had it.

Exit PARMENON.

DEMEAS.
Where do you think you're off to, you little devil?
Grab him.
　　'Oh citadel of Cecrops' land
　　Outstretch'd expanse of Heaven's band'.
What are you on about, Demeas? You're raving,
numbskull. Control. Get a grip on yourself.
　　There. Moschion has done nothing to harm you.

An enigmatic thing to say in the circumstances, you
might think, gentlemen, but true. Had be done what
330   he has done voluntarily, or in an uncontrollable
passion, or even out of spite, he would still be in the
same frame of mind and he would be trying to
brazen it out. But he's obviously in the clear.

The proposed marriage delighted him, not, as I
assumed at the time, because of love or anything like
that, but so as to escape the clutches of this Helen of
Troy of mine. Whatever happened, the fault was
hers. No doubt about that. She'll have caught him
when he was the worse for wear. 'Strong drink and
young blood have much to answer for', especially
340   with a little encouragement.

I still can't fathom how a lad who seemed so
restrained and so reasonable with everyone else
could treat his father like this. I don't care if he was
adopted ten times over, natural son or not, it's
character that counts. I look to nothing else. The
woman's a whore, an infection. Well, what of it? She
won't get round me. Be a man, Demeas. Govern
350   your passions. Fall out of love. And as far as
possible, hush up the whole business. For
Moschion's sake. Pitch her out the house. Oh my
lovely Samian girl. To hell with her. You've got your
excuse. She wouldn't get rid of the baby. That's all
anyone needs to know. 'Though hard be the task,
keep a stiff upper lip'.

Enter COOK.

COOK.

He must be out here, is he? Oy, Parmenon. Damn it,
he's done a runner on me. Fat help he was.

DEMEAS.

Get out the way, will you?

Exit DEMEAS.

COOK.

360   Dear, oh dear. What's all this, then? Some mad old

fellow just rushed indoors. What's his problem?
Why should I bother? Off his head clearly. Nothing
wrong with his lungs though. Hang on. All my
dishes are out. He'll smash the lot. Fine thing that
would be. There's a door slamming. Oh, you can rot
in hell, Parmenon, for bringing me on this job.
Whew. I need a breather.

Enter DEMEAS *and* CHRYSIS.

DEMEAS.
Be off with you. Do you hear?

CHRYSIS.
Where on earth am I to go?

DEMEAS.
You can go to hell, as far as I'm concerned.

CHRYSIS.
This is terrible.

DEMEAS.
Terrible, yes. Tears too? Tragic. I'll soon stop   370
you . . .

CHRYSIS.
Stop me what?

DEMEAS.
Nothing. You've got the child, you've got the old
woman. Now, clear off.

CHRYSIS.
All because I kept the baby?

DEMEAS.
Amongst other things.

CHRYSIS.
What other things?

DEMEAS.
Because of that.

COOK.
So that's what all the excitement's about.

CHRYSIS.

I don't understand.

DEMEAS.

You didn't appreciate when you were well off, did
you?

CHRYSIS.

Didn't appreciate? What are you talking about?

DEMEAS.

You came to this house with the clothes you stood
up in. You know what I'm talking about. One thin
frock.

CHRYSIS.

So?

DEMEAS.

I was everything to you. You were nothing.

CHRYSIS.

Who's nothing now?

DEMEAS.

380   Don't bandy words with me, Chrysis. You have
your own things, You can keep the slaves and the
jewellery. Now, out of my house.

COOK.

It's a very angry man we've got here. I'll have a
word. Excuse me, sir . . .

DEMEAS.

Are you addressing me?

COOK.

Don't bite.

DEMEAS.

Any girl would jump at what I can offer and thank
God for it.

COOK.

What's he on about?

DEMEAS.

You've got the baby. That's what you were after.

COOK.

> Not been bitten yet. Try again. (*Interrupting them.*)
> All the same . . .

DEMEAS.

> If you say another word to me, I'll punch your head
> in.

COOK.

> Quite right. Absolutely. Well, then. I'll be back off
> indoors.

> *Exit* COOK.

DEMEAS.

> Something special, are you? You'll soon find out   390
> how you rate in the city. Ten drachmas a go and a
> free dinner. Till you die of drink. If you don't like the
> idea of that, then starve. You'll learn. Nobody
> quicker. And you'll realise what a mistake you
> made. Just keep out of my way.

> *Exit* DEMEAS.

CHRYSIS.

> What a disaster. This is awful.

> *Enter* NIKERATOS.

NIKERATOS.

> That sheep will provide everything we require for
> the gods and goddesses: blood, nice gall-bladder,   400
> great big spleen, just what the Olympians ordered.
> I'll parcel up bits for my friends and I'll get what's
> left – the skin. Gracious me, what's this? That's
> never Chrysis standing by the door and in tears. It's
> her alright. Whatever's the matter?

CHRYSIS.

> He's thrown me out. That precious friend of yours.
> That good enough for you?

NIKERATOS.

> Good lord. Demeas has?

CHRYSIS.
> Yes.

NIKERATOS.
> Whatever for?

CHRYSIS.
> Because of the baby.

NIKERATOS.
410   Heavens. Well yes, I had heard from the women
> that you had kept it and were going to bring it up
> yourself. Damn fool thing to do but, there you go,
> he's a good-natured fellow.

CHRYSIS.
> He didn't seem to mind at first. Only later.

NIKERATOS.
> Just now?

CHRYSIS.
> One minute he was telling me to make wedding
> preparations for Moschion, the next he came rush-
> ing in like a lunatic and threw me out.

NIKERATOS.
> He's sickening for something. An insalubrious place
> the Black Sea. Come on. We'll go and see my wife.
> Cheer up. Nothing to fret over. Give him a little time
420   to think it all out and he'll come to his senses.

Exeunt NIKERATOS *and* CHRYSIS.

CHORAL INTERLUDE.

ACT 4

Enter NIKERATOS, *talking to his off-stage wife.*

NIKERATOS.
> Woman, you'll be the death of me. I'll go and see
> him this minute. I wouldn't have had this happen.
> Not for money, I wouldn't. Oh dear no. Right in the

middle of the wedding. It's not a good omen. This girl thrown out of his house, coming into mine. Then there's the baby. Tears. Commotion amongst the women. And Demeas. What a shitty way to behave. Lord knows, he'll regret being so thoughtless.

Enter MOSCHION.

MOSCHION.
Will the sun never set? How shall I put it? Night has forgot itself, seeming always afternoon. I think I'll have a shower. I've had two already. What else is there to do?

NIKERATOS.
Moschion. I'm glad I've found you. 430

MOSCHION.
Can we start the wedding? I met Parmenon in the market and he told me it's all set. Can I go and see your daughter yet?

NIKERATOS.
You don't know what's happened ?

MOSCHION.
No. What?

NIKERATOS.
What indeed? Some unpleasantness, all quite inexplicable.

MOSCHION.
Heavens. What unpleasantness? I don't know anything about any unpleasantness.

NIKERATOS.
It's Chrysis. I'm sorry, dear boy, but she's just been hoofed out by your father.

MOSCHION.
That's dreadful.

NIKERATOS.
Nevertheless, it's what happened.

MOSCHION.
Whatever for?

NIKERATOS.
Because of the baby.

MOSCHION.
Where is she now?

NIKERATOS.
She's with us.

MOSCHION.
This is a terrible thing to happen. Quite incredible.

NIKERATOS.
If you think it's so terrible . . .

Enter DEMEAS.

DEMEAS.
440   Give me a stick and I'll give you something to weep about. What is all this nonsense? Why doesn't someone give a hand to the cook? Of course it's a lamentable bloody occasion. A great loss to the household. Obviously.

Lord Apollo, greetings. We ask thy blessing on this wedding and grant us thy benevolence.
I intend going through with it, gentlemen, biting back my fury, but I am going through with the wedding.

And, please, Lord, keep an eye on me and see I don't give the game away and let me sing the wedding-hymn without choking. Even though I'll
450   never see her again.

NIKERATOS.
You first, Moschion. After you.

MOSCHION.
Yes, alright. Father. Father, why are doing this?

DEMEAS.
Doing what, Moschion?

MOSCHION.

What do you mean 'what'? Why has Chrysis left?
Tell me.

DEMEAS.

A deputation. This is too much. That's my business,
damn it. It has nothing to do with you. What
nonsense is this? It's dreadful. They're ganging up
on me.

MOSCHION.

What did you say?

DEMEAS.

I was right. It's obvious. Or why take her side when
he should have been relieved to get rid of her?

MOSCHION.

What do you think your friends will say?

DEMEAS.

My friends, Moschion, will, I expect . . . Let me   460
finish.

MOSCHION.

It would be inhuman to do so.

DEMEAS.

You think you can stop me?

MOSCHION.

Yes, I do.

DEMEAS.

This is beyond the pale. Before was bad enough. But
this . . .

MOSCHION.

'Anger and haste hinder good counsel'.

NIKERATOS.

He's right there, Demeas.

MOSCHION.

Nikeratos. Go on in and tell her to hurry back home.

DEMEAS.

Moschion. Will you allow me? Allow me,

Moschion. And for the third time. I know everything.

MOSCHION.

Everything about what?

DEMEAS.

I don't want to discuss it.

MOSCHION.

You have to discuss it, father.

DEMEAS.

Have to, do I? Am I or am I not master in my own house?

MOSCHION.

One favour, that's all.

DEMEAS.

470

What sort of favour do you fancy? How would it suit you if I were to leave home and let you two get on with it. Oh, I'll arrange the wedding to Plangon while I'm at it. Do, please, let me make the arrangements for the wedding.

MOSCHION.

Well, thank you. But we must have Chrysis there too.

DEMEAS.

Chrysis!

MOSCHION.

I'm doing this all for you.

DEMEAS.

Couldn't be more blatant. Ye gods, I told you it was a conspiracy. I think I shall explode.

MOSCHION?

What are you talking about?

DEMEAS.

You want me to spell it out to you?

MOSCHION.

Alright.

DEMEAS.
Come over here.

MOSCHION.
Tell me.

DEMEAS.
Very well, then. I'll tell you. The baby. I know it's yours. I heard everything from one of your co-conspirators. Parmenon. So don't play games with me.

MOSCHION.
Well, if I'm the father, what have you got against Chrysis?

DEMEAS.
Whose fault is it then? Yours?

MOSCHION.
I don't see where she comes into it.   480

DEMEAS.
Don't you? Have you no conscience, the pair of you?

MOSCHION.
What are you shouting about?

DEMEAS.
What am I shouting about? You blackguard. You dare ask me that? Tell me then. Do you accept the entire responsibility? Have you the nerve to look me in the eye and tell me that?. Do I mean nothing to you?

MOSCHION.
Why are you saying that?

DEMEAS.
You have to ask?

MOSCHION.
Father, it's not that bad. Thousands of people have done it.

DEMEAS.
Brazen. Here, now, with witnesses present. Who is

the mother of that child? You tell Nikeratos if you
don't think it's 'that bad'.

MOSCHION.

Of course it would be wrong to tell him like this.
He'll be furious when he finds out.

NIKERATOS.

You monster, you. I'm beginning to work out what's
going on. The hypocrisy of it.

MOSCHION.

490   Now I have had it.

DEMEAS.

Begin to see, do you, Nikeratos?

NIKERATOS.

What dreadful dole is here? The enseamed bed of
Tereus, the stewed corruption of Oedipus, the nasty
sty of Thyestes. Worse.

MOSCHION.

Who? Me?

NIKERATOS.

You dared do this dreadful deed, dare did you?
Now, Demeas, put on the wrath of Amyntor and
blind the brute.

DEMEAS.

500   It's your fault that he found out.

NIKERATOS.

Is anyone safe? Have you no self-control? And I'm
expected to give you my daughter's hand? Why, I'd
rather – I don't want to tempt providence – I'd
sooner marry her to a bigamist. What an unmiti-
gated catastrophe.

DEMEAS.

It's me who's been wronged, you know, but at least I
kept it to myself.

NIKERATOS.

You've a slave mentality, Demeas. If it was my nest

he'd fouled, he'd never have done it a second time,
and nor would his mate. If it had been a tart of mine,
I'd have sold her off tomorrow and disinherited my
son while I was at it. It'd have been the talk of the
town in every barber's shop and every arcade. From   510
dawn to dusk everybody would have been saying
what a fine fellow Nikeratos was, putting his son on
a murder charge.

MOSCHION.
Murder charge?

NIKERATOS.
I'd call it murder if someone treated me like that.

MOSCHION.
All this has worn me out, God help me. I'm numb.

NIKERATOS.
To cap it all, I've welcomed the perpetrator into my
own home.

DEMEAS.
Then throw her out, Nikeratos, I beg of you. Share
my shame, like a good friend.

NIKERATOS.
If I as much as set eyes on her, I'll explode. Why are
you staring at me, you savage, you sex-starved
Thracian? Get out of my way.

Exit NIKERATOS.

MOSCHION.
Father, for God's sake listen to me.   520

DEMEAS.
I will not listen to anything.

MOSCHION.
Not even if I tell you that none of this is what you
think. I've just realised what's happening.

DEMEAS.
Not what I think?

MOSCHION.

It's not Chrysis who's the mother of that child she
was nursing. She was pretending it was hers to do
me a favour.

DEMEAS.

What are you talking about?

MOSCHION.

It's the truth.

DEMEAS.

In what way to do you a favour?

MOSCHION.

I didn't want to tell you, but 'The lesser fault the
greater doth displace', as you'll see if you only let me
explain.

DEMEAS.

You'll be the death of me if you don't.

MOSCHION.

The baby belongs to Nikeratos' daughter, to Plangon – and to me. That's what I didn't want to tell
you.

DEMEAS.

But how?

MOSCHION.

It just happened.

DEMEAS.

530   Don't try and hoodwink me now.

MOSCHION.

You want proof? What'd be the point of lying about
it?

DEMEAS.

None, I suppose. Ah, there's the door.

Enter NIKERATOS.

NIKERATOS.

Worse and worse and worse. I went into the house.

What spectacle confronted me? I came straight out
again, struck to the quick by what I could least have
expected.

DEMEAS.
What can he mean?

NIKERATOS.
I found my daughter with a baby, giving it her tit.

DEMEAS.
Really?

MOSCHION.
Father, you hear that?

DEMEAS.
Moschion. You were not to blame. It was my fault
entirely for believing you capable of such a thing.

NIKERATOS.
Demeas, I appeal to you.

MOSCHION.
Time for me to be off.

DEMEAS.
Don't worry.

MOSCHION.
I'd sooner die than face him.

Exit MOSCHION.

DEMEAS.
Whatever's the matter?

NIKERATOS.
Giving the baby a tit.   540
I just saw her, my daughter, in my house.

DEMEAS.
Probably a joke.

NIKERATOS.
It was no joke. As soon as she saw me, she collapsed
in a heap.

DEMEAS.
  She probably thought . . .

NIKERATOS.
  What's all this 'probably' all the time?

DEMEAS.
  I feel that I'm responsible for this.

NIKERATOS.
  What are you talking about?

DEMEAS.
  It's hard to credit what you say.

NIKERATOS.
  I saw it.

DEMEAS.
  You must have made a mistake.

NIKERATOS.
  Every word is true, I tell you. I'd better go back.

DEMEAS.
  Most peculiar. Hang on a moment, old chap.

  Exit NIKERATOS.

  Oh, he's gone. What a turnaround. That has torn it.
  When he finds out the truth, God help us, he'll hit
  the roof, shouting and screaming. What an uncivi-
  lised fellow he is, a shit-taster, a real law unto
550 himself.
       How could I have entertained such an idea?
  What a filthy mind. Death's more than I deserve, I
  swear it. Lord, what a bellowing. That's Nikeratos
  alright. Calling for fire. Says he's going to barbecue
  the baby. My grandson and I'll see it toasted.
  Another bang on the door. The man's a whirlwind, a
  positive dervish.

  Re-enter NIKERATOS.

NIKERATOS.
  Demeas, it's a conspiracy. Chrysis is conspiring
  against me and doing all sorts of terrible things.

DEMEAS.
What do you mean?

NIKERATOS.
She's told my wife not to admit to anything. My
daughter too. Now she's seized the baby and refuses
to hand it over. So don't be surprised if I kill her with   560
my bare hands.

DEMEAS.
With your bare hands?

NIKERATOS.
She knows everything.

DEMEAS.
Nikeratos, you can't.

NIKERATOS.
I thought I'd let you know in advance.

Exit NIKERATOS.

He's having a brainstorm. There he goes again.
What's a fellow to do in a mess like this? I've never
known anything like it. It's chaos. Plain, unvar-
nished truth, I think. That's the answer. God
almighty. The door again.

Enter CHRYSIS *with the baby.*

CHRYSIS.
What can I do? How can I escape? He'll take the
child from me.

DEMEAS.
Chrysis. Over here.

CHRYSIS.
Who's that?

DEMEAS.
Inside. Hurry.

Re-enter NIKERATOS.

NIKERATOS.
Where are you? Where've you got to?

DEMEAS.

570   Oh, Lord. Hand-to-hand combat this time, I think. Is there anything you want? After someone, are you?

NIKERATOS.

Now Demeas. Out my way. Let me have that baby and we'll start listening to what the women have got to say.

DEMEAS.

Absolutely not.

NIKERATOS.

You're threatening me.

DEMEAS.

Yes, I am.

NIKERATOS.

Right, then. Take that.

DEMEAS.

Chrysis. Run. He's stronger than me.

Exit CHRYSIS.

NIKERATOS.

You hit me first. I've got witnesses.

DEMEAS.

What about you? Taking a stick to an independent woman and chasing her.

NIKERATOS.

Perjurer.

DEMEAS.

Same to you with knobs on.

NIKERATOS.

The baby. Bring me the baby.

DEMEAS.

Ha, ha. It's my baby.

NIKERATOS.

It is not your baby.

DEMEAS.
  Mine.

NIKERATOS.
  Help. Someone.

DEMEAS.
  Shout your head off.

NIKERATOS.
  I'm off indoors to murder my wife.   580

DEMEAS.
  What am I going to do? This is frightful. I must stop
  him. Where do you think you're off to? Stay here.

NIKERATOS.
  Take your hands off me.

DEMEAS.
  Get a grip on yourself.

NIKERATOS.
  You do me wrong, Demeas. It's perfectly obvious,
  you're in the plot too.

DEMEAS.
  Then allow me to put you in the picture and don't
  take it out on your wife.

NIKERATOS.
  That son of yours has made a fool of me, hasn't he?

DEMEAS.
  What nonsense you do talk. He'll stick by the girl.
  It's not what you think. Come on. Walk with me a
  little.

NIKERATOS.
  Walk?

DEMEAS.
  And pull yourself together. Now, Nikeratos. You
  know that old play, don't you, where Zeus is
  transformed into a shower of gold and seeps through   590
  the roof so he can screw the girl?

NIKERATOS.
What about it?

DEMEAS.
That's just the point. Maybe we ought to anticipate any contingency. Maybe you should make sure that your roof hasn't got a leak.

NIKERATOS.
It's got dozens of them. What on earth has that got to do with anything?

DEMEAS.
That's Zeus, isn't it? Sometimes a shower of gold. Sometimes a shower of rain. You follow? That's the thing. Didn't take long to work that one out, did it?

NIKERATOS.
Are you kidding?

DEMEAS.
Absolutely not. Kid you? Me? You're no worse a man than Acrisius was, I think. And if Zeus found his daughter acceptable, then yours . . .

NIKERATOS.
Damn me if it isn't Moschion making me look an idiot.

DEMEAS.
He'll marry Plangon. Don't worry about it. But I'm telling you, this is a wonderful thing.
There are thousands of people who are wandering about in public whose fathers are gods. What about Chaerephon who's always at parties but never brings a bottle? Only the Almighty could get away with it.

NIKERATOS.
Perhaps you're right. Tell me what to do, I don't want to fight with you over something so trivial.

DEMEAS.
Good thinking, Nikeratos. Then there's Androcles.

600

How old must he be? Always jogging. Plenty of boyfriends. Not one grey hair on his head. He'd rather die with his throat slit than turn white. I'd call that divine, wouldn't you?

Off you go and say your prayers. Burn a bit of incense and have a sacrifice. Moschion will come and fetch Plangon presently.   610

NIKERATOS.
I suppose I have to . . .

DEMEAS.
Of course you do.

NIKERATOS.
If she was taken . . .

DEMEAS.
That's enough. Go and get ready.

NIKERATOS.
Yes. I'll go and get ready.

DEMEAS.
So will I.

NIKERATOS.
Yes. You get ready as well.

DEMEAS.
What a good idea.

Exit NIKERATOS.

And thank God that all my suspicions proved ill-founded.

Exit DEMEAS.

> *CHORAL INTERLUDE.*

ACT 5

Enter MOSCHION.

MOSCHION.

620

At first I was relieved just to be exonerated from a false accusation and thought how lucky I'd been to get away with it. Now I've had time to mull it over and see the implications, I'm absolutely fuming. It makes me furious that my father could even have suspected me of such behaviour. If it wasn't for the position in which Plangon finds herself and all the problems to which I've been subjected, ethical, physical, temporal and natural, he'd never get away with such an accusation. I'd be off, away from Athens, and join up as a mercenary somewhere like Bactria or Caria. But I can't do the brave thing and all because of you, dearest Plangon. I'm in love and love overrules better judgement.

630

I still can't get over the dishonourable, the disreputable, the despicable opinion of me he has demonstrated. I think I should put the wind up him a little, even if I only *tell* him that I'm going to leave the country. If nothing else, he'll think twice before levelling accusations at me in future. Here's Parmenon, the right man at the right time, for once.

640

Enter PARMENON.

PARMENON.

That was so stupid. Hell's teeth. What a brainless, childish thing to do. I hadn't done anything, but I ran away from my master because I got scared. And what crime have I committed? Let us investigate point by point. One. The boy Moschion does what he shouldn't with a free girl. You can't blame Parmenon for that. She gets pregnant. Not guilty. The baby comes into our house. He brought it, not me. A member of the household claims it as hers. What did Parmenon do wrong? Nothing. So why

650

did you run off, you silly coward? It's pathetic. He
did threaten to mark me for life. Yes, that's what it
boils down to. It makes no odds whether I'm in the
right or not. One way or another, I'll catch it.

MOSCHION.
Hey.

PARMENON.
Hello there.

MOSCHION.
No messing about. Just get indoors, quick.

PARMENON.
What for?

MOSCHION.
Fetch my greatcoat and sword.

PARMENON.
A sword? You?

MOSCHION.
Get a move on.   660

PARMENON.
What for?

MOSCHION.
Do it. There's no need for a song and dance.

PARMENON.
What's going on?

MOSCHION.
If I have to get the whip . . .

PARMENON.
No, no. I'm on my way.

MOSCHION.
Then what are you waiting for?

Exit PARMENON.

Father will come out. Then, of course, he'll beg me
to stay. I'll let him beg for a bit. Serve him right.

Then, at a moment of my choosing, I'll let him
persuade me. I'll have to be convincing, though. I
wish I were a better actor. There's the door. He's
coming.

Re-enter PARMENON.

PARMENON.

670   You've been overtaken by events.
Your information's totally out of date which is why
you're getting into such a tizzy over nothing.

MOSCHION.

Haven't you got my things?

PARMENON.

Look, they're starting the wedding. The wine's
mixed. Incense burning.
'Upon such sacrifices, my master,
The Gods themselves throw incense.'

MOSCHION.

What about my things?

PARMENON.

Everything's ready except you. They've been waiting for you for ages. Go and get the girl. It's all
worked out fine. Nobody's annoyed with you. Cheer
up. What more do you want?

MOSCHION.

Order me about, would you, you devil? (*Hits him.*)

PARMENON.

Ow. Moschion, what did you do that for?

MOSCHION.

Get inside and fetch me what I asked for. Fast.

PARMENON.

My lip's bleeding.

MOSCHION.

680   And you're still talking?

PARMENON.

I'm going. I'm going. I've landed in it this time.

MOSCHION.
You're still here.

PARMENON.
The wedding really is on, you know.

MOSCHION.
Still on about that? Tell me something new.

Exit PARMENON.

That'll bring him out. But what am I going to do, gentlemen, if he doesn't beg me to stay? What if he gets angry and lets me go? What'll I do then? He wouldn't. Would he? What if he does? Anything can happen and I'll look ridiculous.

Re-enter PARMENON.

PARMENON.
There. Coat. Sword. Take them.

MOSCHION.
Bring them here, then. Anybody . . . notice you? Anybody inside?

PARMENON.
Nobody.

MOSCHION.
Ah, nobody. Nobody at all?

PARMENON.
I told you.

MOSCHION.
Why did you tell me that? To hell with you.

PARMENON.
Off you trot. Anywhere you want. You're making a fool of yourself.

Enter DEMEAS.

DEMEAS.
Well, where is he then?   690
Tell me. My boy. What is all this?

PARMENON.

> Off you go. Get a move on.

DEMEAS.

> Why are you wearing your coat? What's the matter?
> You're not leaving, are you?

PARMENON.

> You can see he is, All ready for the road. I'd better
> go and warn the family. I'm on my way.

Exit PARMENON.

DEMEAS.

> Oh Moschion. You're upset and I love you for it. I
> can't say I blame you when I made such a ground-
> less accusation against you. I was wrong. All I can
> do is ask you to consider this. Even in bad times, I'm
> still your father. I took you in when you were a baby
> and I've brought you up. If your life has had some
> 700   joy in it, give me credit for that and balance it
> against the pain I've caused, as a son should. I
> blamed you for something you never did. That was
> unfair. I shouldn't have done it. I must have been
> out of my mind. That's the way things go. I was
> trying to protect your reputation in the eyes of the
> world, so I confided in noone. And all along I had
> the wrong end of the stick.
>
> But I never said a word that an enemy could gloat
> over. What you're doing is broadcasting this mis-
> take of mine and telling the world what a fool I've
> 710   been. That's not worthy of you, Moschion. Don't
> allow the one day in your life when I let you down
> drive out the memory of the past. There's more I
> could say but, never mind. Grudging obedience
> won't do, you know. A father needs respect.

Enter NIKERATOS.

NIKERATOS.

> Don't hold me back. Everything's ready. Libations,
> sacrifices, ceremony. All we need is him, if he ever

deigns to come in, so the girl's got someone for me to
give her to. What's going on?

DEMEAS.

I don't know. Damned if I do.

NIKERATOS.

How can you not know? That's his greatcoat. He's
planning to leave. It's obvious.

DEMEAS.

That's what he says.

NIKERATOS.

Says that, does he? And who's going to let him go, a
self-confessed fornicator, caught in the act? I'll bind
you over, young man, and quick about it.

MOSCHION.

Yes. You tie me up. Try it.

NIKERATOS.

Oh, you do talk rubbish. Put your sword away, will
you.

DEMEAS.

Do put it away, Moschion, I implore you. Stop
getting him excited.

MOSCHION.

Oh, very well, then.   720
Seeing as you beg me. You win.

NIKERATOS.

Seeing as we beg you? Come here.

MOSCHION.

Are you going to tie me up?

DEMEAS.

No, no he isn't. Go and fetch the bride.

NIKERATOS.

Are you sure?

DEMEAS.

Yes. Yes, of course.

Exit NIKERATOS.

MOSCHION.

If you'd behaved like this in the first place, Father, we could have done without the moralising.

Re-enter NIKERATOS *with* PLANGON *followed by* CHRYSIS *and* MYRRHINE.

NIKERATOS.

You first. Out you go.

Before witnesses I bestow this child upon you for the procreation of legitimate children, with all my worldly goods as a dowry, but not until I'm dead, which may never happen if I live for ever.

MOSCHION.

I hold her. I accept her. I love her.

DEMEAS.

Now all that is left is Moschion's ablutions. Chrysis, fetch the women, a water-carrier and a flute-player. Someone bring a torch and garlands and we'll all join the procession.

MOSCHION.

They're here already.

DEMEAS.

A garland for your head. Now smarten youself up a bit.

MOSCHION.

Anything you say, father.

DEMEAS.

Handsome boys, young men and old, gentlemen of the audience, your applause, please, that lovely sound which signifies the favour of Dionysus. And may the blessed goddess, Victory incarnate, judge of our splendid drama competitions. look with favour on my choruses, now and always.

END

A Note on the Translators

KENNETH McLEISH'S books include *The Theatre of Aristophanes*, *Shakespeare's People A-Z* and *The Good Reading Guide*. His original films and plays include *Just Do It*, *Tony*, *Vice at the Vicarage* (for Frankie Howerd) and *Omma* (commissioned by the Young Vic and premiered there in 1994). His translations include plays by all the extant Greek and Roman dramatists, and by Ibsen, Feydeau, Labiche, Goldoni and Strindberg. His translation of Sophocles' *Electra* was directed by Deborah Warner at the RSC in 1989; his version of Ibsen's *Peer Gynt* was directed by Declan Donnellan at the Royal National Theatre in 1990; his adaptation of Feydeau's *Pig in a Poke* was toured by the Oxford Stage Company in 1992 and his version of Strindberg's *The Great Highway* was premièred at the Gate Theatre, London in 1993.

J MICHAEL WALTON worked in the professional theatre as an actor and director before joining the University of Hull, where he is Professor and Head of the Drama Department. He has published three books on Greek theatre, *Greek Theatre Practice*, *The Greek Sense of Theatre: Tragedy Reviewed*, and *Living Greek Theatre: A Handbook of Classical Performance and Modern Production*. He has also published in a number of areas of more modern British and European theatre, is the editor of *Craig on Theatre* and General Editor of Methuen Classical Drama in Translation.

Methuen World Classics

Aeschylus (two volumes)
Jean Anouilh
John Arden (two volumes)
Arden & D'Arcy
Aristophanes
  (two volumes)
Aristophanes & Menander
Peter Barnes (two volumes)
Brendan Behan
Aphra Behn
Edward Bond (four volumes)
Bertolt Brecht (four volumes)
Howard Brenton
  (two volumes)
Büchner
Bulgakov
Calderón
Anton Chekhov
Caryl Churchill
  (two volumes)
Noël Coward (five volumes)
Sarah Daniels (two volumes)
Eduardo De Filippo
David Edgar
  (three volumes)
Euripides (three volumes)
Dario Fo (two volumes)
Michael Frayn
  (two volumes)
Max Frisch
Gorky
Harley Granville Barker
  (two volumes)

Henrik Ibsen (six volumes)
Lorca (three volumes)
David Mamet
Marivaux
Mustapha Matura
David Mercer
  (two volumes)
Arthur Miller
  (four volumes)
Anthony Minghella
Molière
Tom Murphy
  (three volumes)
Peter Nichols (two volumes)
Clifford Odets
Joe Orton
Louise Page
A. W. Pinero
Luigi Pirandello
Stephen Poliakoff
  (two volumes)
Terence Rattigan
Ntozake Shange
Sophocles (two volumes)
Wole Soyinka
David Storey (two volumes)
August Strindberg
  (three volumes)
J. M. Synge
Ramón del Valle-Inclán
Frank Wedekind
Oscar Wilde

Methuen Modern Plays

include work by

Jean Anouilh
John Arden
Margaretta D'Arcy
Peter Barnes
Brendan Behan
Edward Bond
Bertolt Brecht
Howard Brenton
Simon Burke
Jim Cartwright
Caryl Churchill
Noël Coward
Sarah Daniels
Nick Dear
Shelagh Delaney
David Edgar
Dario Fo
Michael Frayn
John Guare
Peter Handke
Jonathan Harvey
Declan Hughes
Terry Johnson

Barrie Keeffe
Stephen Lowe
Doug Lucie
John McGrath
David Mamet
Arthur Miller
Mtwa, Ngema & Simon
Tom Murphy
Peter Nichols
Joe Orton
Louise Page
Luigi Pirandello
Stephen Poliakoff
Franca Rame
David Rudkin
Willy Russell
Jean-Paul Sartre
Sam Shepard
Wole Soyinka
Theatre Workshop
Sue Townsend
Timberlake Wertenbaker
Victoria Wood